Mykonos

A MEMOIR BY NANCY RAEBURN

Minnesota Voices Project Number 51

NEW RIVERS PRESS 1992

The publication of *Mykonos: A Memoir* has been made possible by generous grants from the Dayton Hudson Foundation and the Metropolitan Regional Arts Council (from an appropriation by the Minnesota Legislature). Additional support has been provided by the Arts Development Fund of the United Arts Council, the First Bank System Foundation, Liberty State Bank, the Star Tribune/Cowles Media Company, the Tennant Company Foundation, and the National Endowment for the Arts (with funds appropriated by the Congress of the United States). New Rivers Press also wishes to acknowledge the Minnesota Non-Profits Assistance Fund for its invaluable support.

New Rivers Press books are distributed by

The Talman Company
150 Fifth Avenue
New York, NY 10011

Bookslinger
2402 University Avenue West
Saint Paul, MN 55114

Mykonos: A Memoir has been manufactured in the United States of America for New Rivers Press, 420 N. 5th Street/Suite 910, Minneapolis, MN 55401 in a first edition of 2,000 copies.

To my brother Jamie's children,
Laurie and Sean

and to the people of Mykonos.

Contents

Acknowledgements

Two of the chapters in *Mykonos: A Memoir* appeared in somewhat different versions in *The House on Via Gombito: Writing by North American Women Abroad* (New Rivers Press).

New Rivers Press and the author gratefully acknowledge Annie Dillard for the use of the passage from *Pilgrim at Tinker Creek* (Harpers Magazine Press, 1974); Rodney Jones for the use of lines from the poem "For the Eating of Swine," (*The Unborn*, Atlantic Monthly Press, 1985); Stanley Kunitz for the use of lines from the poem "The Layers" (*The Poems of Stanley Kunitz, 1928-1978*, Little, Brown & Company, 1979); and Catherine Ponder for the use of the passage from *Dynamic Laws of Healing* (DeVorss & Co., 1972). Also, *The Way of the Sufi* by Indries Shah (Dutton & Co., 1970) and *The Last Unicorn* by Peter Beagle (Ballantine Books, 1968).

The author would also like to express her gratitude to all who provided help and encouragement in the writing and production of this book with special thanks to Alvin Greenberg, whose guidance nurtured its earliest drafts, and to Roger Blakely for his skilled editing of the final phases.

In order to protect the identity of some of the people mentioned, the author has changed some names and details.

*"I love delicacy, and I believe all
bright and beautiful things spring
from desire of the sun."*
—Sappho
6th century B.C.

Preface

I LIVED ON AN ISLAND ONCE IN THE MIDDLE OF THE
Aegean Sea. As Greek islands go, this one is small – ten square miles
perhaps, with a population of about 4,000 souls. A small mountain
guards its desolate north side, and a spine of craggy hills shields from
wind a wide, fertile valley along the southern coast. For half the year
it rains and everything turns green. The rest of the time its climate
is arid and vegetation sparse, a warm ochre landscape shimmering in
the heat of full summer.

The population is concentrated in two towns. The small village of
Ano Mera in the center of the island is inhabited by farmers mostly,
a few tradespeople and a smattering of monks and nuns from a nearby
monastery and convent. Then there is the *hóra* or main town,
whitewashed and gleaming in the sunlight. Like an ancient theater,
it sweeps down from the surrounding hills to the small circular harbor
below. Merchants, craftspeople, and fishermen live there, who each
summer sacrifice every spare bed and corner to the thriving tourist
industry.

I discovered the island of Mykonos in 1967 on my first trip to Greece.
I stayed there ten lazy and sun-washed days in a *pensione* before moving on to Crete on a pilgrimage to the birthplace of Nikos Kazantzakis. His vivid and passionate writings had fueled my desire to see
the country that both nurtured and spurned him. Two years later I
was back on Mykonos, this time for a month, to paint under the
tutelage of Luis Orozco, a Mexican artist who had been living there
with his family for many years. A year at the School of the Museum
of Fine Arts in Boston followed. Then in May 1970 I was able to return
for a third visit.

This time I intended to remain there and paint through September. But as the hot winds of August and throngs of tourists began to subside, the island became so tranquil and beautiful that I longed to stay on through the winter. Since I could supplement a small inheritance with painting sales, I was confident of managing financially. By western standards, everything, from bread at ten cents a loaf to the monthly rental of my first house at eighteen dollars, was remarkably cheap. I gave up my apartment in Cambridge, Massachusetts, and friends stored my belongings until I could return the following autumn to sort them out.

Little did I know then that the decision to stay the winter – so casually arrived at – would herald a sojourn lasting a little over ten years of my life.

Chapter One
The House

*"And of all these things the
Albino Whale was a symbol. Wonder
ye then at the fiery hunt?"*
— Herman Melville

MY HOUSE THAT FIRST SUMMER AND WINTER WAS THE second story of a duplex in the heart of the *hóra*. It was a drafty old dwelling with sixteen-foot ceilings supported by wide arches. The original wood floor had been replaced by cement, which made my feet ache in the unheated dampness of that first winter. By December I was forced to abandon the dank chill of the lofty main room and move into the smaller back bedroom that I used as a studio. French doors led out to the roof of the lower house, which provided an ideal sun trap, reflecting heat off the adjoining white walls back into the room. There I settled near my propane gas heater and tea kettle surrounded by piles of books and skeins of homespun wool from which I crocheted numerous bags, hats, and an occasional sweater. I had lots of visitors — hardy friends who braved with me our first winter without central heating and the usual distractions of the American lifestyle. As rain pelted down and the narrow streets ran rivers, I poured endless mugs of hot tea while we traded the latest town gossip and probed the timeless mysteries of life, death, and love — ideas that stoked our imaginations and warmed us almost as much as the first warm and steady sun of April.

Besides warming our bones, however, the arrival of April also meant open doors and windows, normally a delightful prospect after having been closed in for six months. But my house was on one of the main streets. Though scarcely eight feet wide, the street still served as the main thoroughfare for small three-wheeled trucks whose high-pitched and deafening roar grossly misrepresented their power. As they strained under loads of bottled water, cartons of olive oil or produce, coils of rope and frantically bleating livestock, the noise of these minuscule delivery trucks fell hard on ears accustomed to the muffled sounds of winter. Rather than endure another summer of such noise pollution that could only increase with the arrival of tourists, I arranged to rent a house in the country over the hill surrounding the *hóra*.

An old farmer, Manolis Asimomitis, was my new landlord, and the house belonged to one of his daughters who lived in the United States. All the land for acres around belonged to his other children and grand-children, and in the year that I was there, what had once been rolling wheatfields became plots of land where, one after the other, his relatives began to build their suburban dream houses. So it wasn't long before a growing need for solitude compelled me to move further out, into another house on a less heavily beaten track.

I lived in this old three-room farmhouse, about a twenty minute walk from the harbor, for eight of my ten years on the island. It had been rented before me by friends who were also painters, so I knew it well, having spent many pleasant afternoons and evenings on its ter-race or within its thick walls on cold winter days. The kindly owner, a diminutive woman named Yiorgia, rented it for a pittance, and it is probably due to that fact as much as to my attachment to island life that I managed to stay as long as I did. Even more, there was a spirit to this house that was unique, and, as artists, my friends and I had come to appreciate the particular qualities of the island's older dwellings.

Those constructed before 1930 seemed to grow right out of the earth. Built long before bulldozers and dynamite could carve flat spaces out of the unruly landscape, these structures had to conform to the land, because the land was not going to conform to them. Some nestled within an outcropping of rock that protected them from the north wind. Others, like mine, occupied a granite plate of gently descending plateaus that signaled the presence of underground water: a good well site. From a distance, against the bright moonlit sky, my house ap-peared to be just another part of the hillside as it tumbled gently down to the fields below. And all around, as far as the eye could see, were garlands of dry-stone walls, some built centuries ago and covered with hoary beards of gray lichen.

Not only did these houses seem to grow out of the land, but they were constructed out of the land as well: the granite stones farmers had cleared from their fields to plant crops, and mud mortar extracted from watering holes dug for livestock. In that great economy of peasants wherever they are found, everything was recycled, including labor.

My house had been built long before the advent of reinforced concrete, a fairly recent innovation in the islands. But its walls were strong enough to withstand almost a century of rain and windlashing and, if maintained well, could last another hundred years. These farmers from the past had been schooled by their fathers, and their fathers before them, in all the skills necessary to sustain life. They understood the principle of triangular strength and applied it to the construction of the buildings that sheltered them and their animals from the elements; the walls of older dwellings, including mine, slanted inward slightly toward the ceiling. This simple formula provided strength without distorting the shape of the room. In fact, an unschooled inhabitant such as I had to be told that the walls were slightly closer to each other near the top than at the floor. Once I saw this, I realized that all the seemingly straight lines were subtly modulated and softened, further enhancing the organic feel of the place. The same spirit that inspired the design of the Parthenon, nearly 2,500 years before, infused the walls of this old farmhouse.

The roof drew from both land and sea for its materials. First, four by four beams had been laid across the width of the house at six-inch intervals. These beams supported a mat of bamboo poles lashed together. Bamboo linked in such a way is very strong and, because it was placed parallel to the lengthwise axis of the house, allowed for the necessary distribution of weight over the ten or twelve beams passing crosswise under it. On top of the bamboo four to six inches of dried seaweed had been spread to provide insulation and also help prevent the next layer, mud, from crumbling into the room after it dried. The six inches of wet mud flattened the seaweed to about two inches, so the roof ended up being some ten inches thick. Then it was plastered and over the years whitewashed countless times as final protection from the elements.

Whitewash, that milky substance made from lime, was the "paint" used by everyone, farmer, fisherman, merchant alike. Every spring I whitewashed the interior walls of the main room and kitchen that composed one wing. The walls in these rooms were covered with so many layers that the whitewash had developed a natural texture mellow and soft enough that it rose and fell in gentle undulations like frosting over the large granite stones it covered. In modern homes this texture is simulated with sophisticated spray blowers that fling the plaster onto the surface in measured blotches or swirls. But the beauty of older walls is the natural flow of plaster over stones.

This texture was visible especially in the clear, oblique light of late afternoon – a light setting off with a special radiance every object in the room. The simple cane-seated straight chair, a copper candlestick gone to a blue-green patina, the striped handwoven bedspread and rugs, a wooden mortar and pestle, the colorful fisherman doll, a collection of stones and shells, paintings – all fit, all were meant to dwell between subtle white walls, reflecting this rare light that amplified their simple beauty.

But best of all, the floors were white! They, too, came from the stones, gravel, and mud of the landscape, and then were swabbed with layer upon layer of whitewash. We all should spend some part of our lives with white floors. Whitewashed walls reflected light and illuminated everything; white floors radiated energy from below and made the room seem cleaner than it might have been. The dust in this house, after all, was white.

White. But not colorless, for all the hues of the spectrum are contained in white. The only thing needed to detect them is the prism provided by the lens of the eye, and all colors, depending on the season or the time of day, will eventually become visible.

The young light of dawn, for example. A normal waking hour for me was half-past seven, but occasionally, for no reason, my eyes would open at five. Wide awake, I'd lie and watch the rosy glow turning gold, emerging from the cool greens and blues of the last retreating shadows of night. For some reason, the changing light often reminded me of music.

This soft emergence of the early dawn in particular recalled an experience as I hurried down a narrow donkey trail on the south side of the island. I had stopped suddenly below an outcropping of rock. A young Greek girl on the terrace of a nearby house had just shaken rugs and was leaning out over the parapet that overlooked the valley tumbling down to the deep blue morning sea. She was singing – clearly and full-voiced and, what lent it its remarkable sound, slightly off-key. To come upon a sound of such unabashed joy when my mind was on my hurrying was like being washed in a sea of the earliest morning's greens and blues. The retreating shadows of night coloring my walls at five o'clock sounded like that young girl's song.

Then there was the white white of mid-afternoon – soundless, except that maybe it buzzed or hissed, searing like a laser, vaporizing everything. Or the hours between five and eight on a summer evening, a light that gave the walls a golden tint, then rose, the opposite of dawn's progression. Their sound would be warm, a full, dark contralto, Mahler's *Songs of the Earth*. And later still, the milk blue walls turning a sinister yellow as they reflected the two-week wax and wane of the moon: Debussy and Berlioz.

Inside these foot-and-a-half thick walls my furnishings were simple. There was a bed facing the doorway, crudely made wooden shelves for clothing, a chest for blankets and off-season clothes. Above it I hung a small bookshelf, and near the door a friend constructed a closet, a rod suspended from two ceiling beams and curtained around. In opposite corners sat two refurbished director's chairs I had salvaged from the sea.

Through a low-hung door and down a half step was the kitchen, a small, square room, whose raised corner fireplace gave the illusion of roundness. One window opened above a makeshift counter, and on its wide sill I stacked the clean dishes where the breeze would dry them in minutes. Another window faced west. Kalliope, the cat, who as a very young kitten showed up on my doorstep one day, loved to sit in that window and preen herself, watching with half-closed eyes the red globe of the sun as it sank into the sea. Near this window a small table and bench served for meals when the weather didn't permit eating on the terrace. A two-burner gas stove and oven met most needs, except for the woodsmoke flavor that fireplace cooking in the winter provided to stews and other slow-cooking dishes. I kept the kitchen water supply in a large clay amphora, dipping it out with an enameled ladle. At night I read by the light of kerosene lamps. And, except for visitors and friends, I lived there alone with a coterie of stray cats and other creatures who sheltered themselves in the walls and ceiling of the old house.

During my first year there, life began to assume an interesting dimension: far from being mistress of this house, I realized I shared it *with* those others, inhabitants who, if I included their ancestors, had lived there much longer than I. I tried to live peacefully and, most important, fearlessly with all of them. So I included in a kind of amnesty the centipedes who lost their grip on the bamboo and dropped onto my bed during the night, the half-dead lizards, mice and snakes Kalliope brought in and the viper, who had wintered behind the paintings stacked in the studio, found one morning coiled groggily in the April sun warming the step. Also, the numerous spiders and their webs, whom I didn't disturb and who normally didn't disturb me, unless one would find its way between my sheets and bite me when I rolled over on *it*.

Then came April when the air was warm and the north breeze dry and fresh, and I would get an urge to clean everything, to dry everything out, to polish and scrub, to repaint and repair. When that great surge of energy and motivation struck, I would set aside one week; the first task was to take a long-handled broom to sweep down the ceiling.

Dust from the beams clouded the air, and a rain of straggly seaweed descended from where it had poked through gaps in the bamboo, bringing with it some of the ancient mud, dry and crumbly. Debris on the floor grew thick and piled up.

I had left the spiders and their webs alone all year, until this one day arrived to divest them of their homes, but not, if I could help it, their lives. As gently as possible I extricated the dust-thickened web of the individual who had been wintering there near the translucent corpse of its mother, long dead after bearing her babies in their tiny cluster of fuzz.

When this spider, who had lived on a diet of flies and gnats into its own wonderful, full-grown selfhood; when this creature, whose ancestors I had been living with peacefully for several (of their) generations; when this creature fell, or was swept out of a dark corner of a cupboard, or from behind the dish cabinet; when it found itself alone, exposed naked near a pile of debris on my white, white floor, what did it do? Over a period of eight spring cleanings I noted three tactics: it might run in any direction, or in several directions, seeking the shelter of dark, shadowy places. Or it might roll itself up in a tight, fuzzy ball and lie still as the fuzzy balls of dusty cobwebs that lay inertly nearby. Or it might simply stay where it had landed, waiting to see what would happen next, totally exposed, vulnerable, perhaps in shock. All of these alternatives – and it is hard not to anthropomorphize here – seemed to be logical responses to the sudden and unexpected change in its situation. The upheaval suffered by a single spider on "Spring Cleaning: Day One" could be tantamount to an earthquake or tornado on human scale.

Those who ran in panic fared the worst. My solution (certainly not the best, but the handiest) was to sweep them one by one into the dustpan and throw them outside over the wall near the house. The spider who ran in fear, who tried to avoid at any cost my gentle nudge into the dustpan, usually ended up getting mangled by my multiple attempts to save it. Sometimes in its wild flight I had to concede that a bad situation was fast becoming worse and tried to guide it back under the shelter of the stove or behind the shelves of pots and pans, diverting it with the cold metal wall of the dustpan smack in its path. Sometimes this approach worked, but usually the spider's frenzy only increased, and it would tear off in another direction, perhaps right into the pile of debris. Dark and smelling of home as it did, this refuge brought only illusory victory. Once there, the spider rolled itself into a protective ball that couldn't be distinguished from the dust balls. Eventually, both spider and dust got emptied into the trash and ended up days later in a plastic bag secured with a twistie, steaming in the sun in an obscure corner of the island dump.

The spider who lived was, ironically, the one who stood still, right out in the open. When the metal of the dustpan and the long bristles of the broom straws approached from either side it didn't move, so I could easily flip it into the pan, run outside and toss it over the wall into a fragrant field of camomile. Salvation, for the spiders anyway, depended on remaining visible, their very vulnerability being their greatest strength.

In June and July came a proliferation of the usual summer insects. Ants engaged most of my energies, since they managed to circumvent every plan concocted to keep them from my food. They nested in the walls of the house, and every year with the first warm weather, resumed their relentless search for sustenance. While most ants seemed indiscriminate in taste, they appeared to share a consistent attraction to sugar and honey. It intrigued me how a scout got the message back to the nest, that it remembered where the cache had been found and could communicate this information to its comrades. I would come home in mid-afternoon or wake in the morning to find an unbroken line extending from the small hole under the kitchen step all the way across the floor and up the opposite wall to a niche where I kept sugar and honey. Another line of them headed back in the opposite direction, touching antennae, perhaps to encourage those moving forward.

Well, it's nothing new; ants are fascinating. They intrigued me with their organization, their devotion to survival, their vast, hungry numbers and, ultimately, by the fact that I couldn't do a thing about them. A sympathetic friend advised me to create a simple barrier of water, much like a moat that protected medieval castles. To do this I was to fill a large washtub one-third full of water and then put a platform of some kind in the middle to store all foods that were particularly vulnerable to ants. When the ants sensed, as they always did, the whereabouts of their favorite comestibles and climbed in a long train up the outside of the tub, over the rim and down again, they were stopped by the water and, so the theory went, would have to turn around and go home again. But, some were pushed into the water by the advancing, hungry throngs behind them, so that in the morning hundreds of tiny black corpses floated in the moat. The system worked – none reached the food – but I abandoned the idea because of the carnage.

It just seemed as if there was nothing to do but surrender. But before I did that, I had one last idea. I put a small plate containing a spoonful of honey on a piece of bread down by the entrance to their nest, off to the side where I wouldn't step on it in the dark. It worked. I gave them everything they needed, and they were satisfied. Every two days I replenished the supply. I was triumphant, until one morning I found their plate of food untouched and the familiar long line stretched across the floor, up the leg of the table and onto its top, where a piece of rice and chicken from the previous night had escaped unwiped in the lamp's dimness.

Something more. All creatures, when their basic needs are satisfied, will seek something more. Manna will not do; they demand quail.

From that time on, whenever anyone asked me about my lifestyle, the subject of food always came up. "Well, what kind of food did you eat out there all alone in that little house?" they asked, as if I'd been marooned on a desert island.

"The same as the ants." I answered.

In this house, even the most frightening occupant of all, because of its vicious sting and repulsive appearance, enjoyed amnesty. A centipede can move very fast on its numerous legs, usually heading for the dark corners of the bedclothes if it has fallen from the ceiling, as often happened. If I didn't move fast, I knew I would never find it and would have to go the rest of the night without sleep, dread of its fierce sting overtaking any decision in this case to be fearless.

Before making my resolution to live and let live, I tried to kill these creatures whenever I found them, both of us in a state of high panic.

I usually went for the dustpan, the only hard, sharp object that I could find on such sudden, wild notice (and which later would become the instrument of questionable salvation for the spider). But centipedes are encased in a segmented shell, the color and strength of a boiled lobster, and were well protected from my blows. Though almost impregnable, they were woundable and, if wounded, emitted a menacing and sickening rattle as they writhed in agony on the floor near my bed. After one too many of these episodes, the centipedes too went into the dustpan, undamaged, very much alive, and over the wall.

The same with the numerous stunned vipers Kalliope brought in to "worry" in the kitchen, and as many of her lizards, mice and birds as I managed to rescue with salvageable life still left in them. There was one exception: a snow white seagull dying on my kitchen floor. Hugh, an American friend, happened to come by just as I was about to dispose of the carcass. Never one to waste anything, he insisted on plucking it. I cooked the bird in a large pot of water and fed the cats for three days.

I hadn't always been so sensitive about killing things, though several times I had done so by accident and felt some remorse. When I was nine, for example, my heel came down on something soft; the gaping mouth of that frog in its agony haunts me to this day, as does the demise of several birds and small animals that connected with my speeding car. Then there were all the mosquitoes and flies. In my life up to that point, I had probably dispatched thousands with bare hand or fly swatter, purposely and with no remorse at all. And imagine all the unseen mass departures inspired by aerosol spray or Clorox bottle. "Killer" could have been my *nom de guerre* because, as far as I was concerned, war it definitely was.

Very early on I learned the axiom that helps make human beings so uncomfortable in the natural world. "It's Them Against Us" is more than an axiom, really; it becomes a way of thinking, of living, and it begins in childhood when our parents teach us to avoid what is harmful. This injunction is sensible enough – indeed necessary – but the problem lies in the definition of harm and what it is, really, that is harmful to us. I killed lots of spiders, because I was afraid of them, afraid they would bite me and hurt me. I killed lots of mosquitoes too, who did bite, but who didn't hurt me all that badly.

But when Kalliope dropped one litter of kittens too many, the question was not one of harm, but inconvenience. Rather than troubling to find homes for them – a difficult task on an island overrun with sickly strays – I had to confront the prospect of killing them too. After all, as Hugh said: cats without homes suffered horrible lives dominated by the constant search for food and the peril of diseases that left their faces half eaten away by a slow, leprous-like putrescence. Much as I hated the prospect of killing the kittens, I had seen enough of these pathetic beasts to be convinced that, in the long run, I'd probably be doing the responsible thing.

So, one terrible day, I reluctantly took Hugh's advice and put them in a plastic bag (which happened to be baby blue) and lay them in a shallow grave I'd dug. My landlord at the time, Barba Manolis, arrived at the end of the crucial hour. We went together to the grave at the back of the house. He nudged the still, blue bundle with his foot. "*Finíto,*" he said. That was that, a simple, effective procedure. But harrowing, nevertheless, for during the hour spent waiting alone in the house, I hadn't dared dwell long on what might be going on inside that bag.

"*Finíto*" I couldn't say quite so easily a year later when Kalliope produced another litter of five kittens, blind, their soft fur roiling as they pumped at her teats in the cardboard box under my bed. This time I decided that if I was going to kill, I had better know exactly what I was doing, and so I eschewed the comfortable anonymity of opaque plastic bags for the honesty of an open bucket of water and two bare hands.

This time another friend, Iraklis, dropped by just at the eleventh hour. I'd been procrastinating all day. Earlier, I'd even tried to buy some chloroform at the pharmacy, but for some reason, the druggist was not permitted to sell it for such purposes. Plucking up all my dignity, I said that I couldn't imagine for what other purpose it would be used, and walked out near tears. I was not looking forward to the water.

After all, I knew these kittens. Almost a week old, their eyes were about to open, and they were beginning to take on individual personalities. I was very attached to their mother and had watched over the birth of each of them. Though Iraklis sympathized, he would not do any killing, he said. He would not leave, however, as I'm sure he wanted to.

Scared as I was, I still thought their deaths would be easy – just one lungful of water and it would be all over. I was not prepared for how hard those tiny creatures would cling to life, for how strong they were. I hadn't expected their anguished cries for help (nor those of Kalliope, locked in the kitchen with one kitten left to suckle). No, not prepared for the endless soft bumping pressure of their heads against the palms of my hands, not expecting the conflict inside me (I could still save them, after all; it wasn't too late). Not prepared for the tears that fell into that churning water when I realized I couldn't lift my hands, couldn't turn back, that I had to finish it, them. Not prepared when it was done to see the soft wisps of mother's milk spill into the water from their open mouths.

That was how it happened; after that I decided to just live, and let live all the creatures who happened to pass through my house. From then on, whenever Kalliope bore another litter, after six weeks I'd put them in a wicker basket with a screen laced over the top and walk into town to find them homes. This was eccentric behavior to most Greeks, such sentimentality about cats. Too many cats were pests and had to be controlled. With no veterinarian on the island, they were right theoretically. But I know even they hated to kill off the young ones and would instead abandon them, only four or five weeks old, behind a wall along a well-traveled donkey path, where their crying might attract the attention of some soft-hearted soul – often a foreigner like me – which was how, in a roundabout way, I'd acquired Kalliope in the first place. If these kittens were not rescued, they would die long, painful deaths of starvation or, more likely, dehydration in the searing white heat of the June sun.

White, the house, the seagull, wisps of milk trailing from mouths of dead kittens; the soft fur on the breast of Kalliope as she purred and nursed her babies, or the paw she pressed against the back of a dazed mouse as she gnawed off its head. White, the lime used in whitewash; horses in the sea in windy August. White, the sky, the sea at midday when every living thing runs for shelter; the linen shroud at wakes. White, a spray of wildflowers that trailed that fall like mother's milk over the graves of dead kittens. White, the Queen Anne's Lace with microcosm-macrocosm message encircling its labial, deep violet center; white, the goats with yellow snake eyes, sheep bleating. White, the moon, the horse one April night in a field of wildflowers; white, silk of the spider patiently wrapping up in sticky strands a struggling centipede ten times its size. White, color of light, color of darkness. White.

Chapter Two
Yiorgos

NO MATTER HOW HE TIMED HIS ARRIVALS, THEY WERE nearly always inappropriate. Like the day I had just packed away all the chores of a morning and was halfway out of the house on my way to town for a bottle of olive oil before the stores closed, and he just appeared, sweating a little under his straw hat, grateful, he said, for a drink of water. Or when he came by the last time, on a Friday: I had finally mustered the nerve to shatter the blankness of that peaceful white canvas that had been sitting all week on the easel. "Anna," his cheerful greeting sounded out near the barn, jarring my concentration like a dissonant flash of cadmium red – or the ring of a telephone, which in the U.S. might have heralded such a visit. But I had no phone, and besides, it was not the custom here on the island to call beforehand. One just simply made room in one's life or at one's table – and cheerfully so – for uninvited guests.

So here he was again, unexpected and for the moment unwelcome, and I thought, most unlike a Greek, oh, no, I can't take the time to visit with Yiorgos; he's simply come at the wrong time. I replaced the brush on my work table and went out on the terrace, barely able to erase the impatience that scored my forehead, intent on sending him "away, away; come again some other day."

But he disarmed me every time, this little man with bandy legs, cane in one hand, wicker basket in the other, full of offerings from his abundant garden – freshly harvested grapes, figs or plums, all dewy and perfect. He had spent an hour selecting them, arranging each fruit just so in the basket and then taken another fifteen minutes crossing fields and high stone walls with all his fleshly and earthly burdens. Now he was here, and I couldn't just take his gifts, which he would insist on leaving with me, and send him back laboring over the walls and fields to his garden cottage another fifteen minutes away. There was something else too, besides guilt, that I was feeling, something about *him*, an unidentified stirring that compelled me to be kind to this man, a sense that his greatest gifts were intangible, richer by far than the succulent contents of the wicker basket.

"*Yiá soū*, Yiorgo!" I called. "How are you, fine? Come in out of the sun and let's have a coffee."

We sat drinking the thick, sweet brew out of cups tiny as those in a child's tea set. "Don't smoke, Anna," he always said when I lit up. "It's not good for you." And behind his words I heard, "It's not right for a lady . . ."

We passed the time exchanging news. In earlier visits Yiorgos had told me the story of his father's death and how at sixteen he'd had to work to support his mother and five unmarried sisters. Life wasn't easy in Greece in the 1920s, so he decided to go to America where he could earn more money. I'd strain to understand his broken English as he talked on, telling of his life in Chicago working as a chef on the Great Northern Railroad.

"I live in jus' about all city in Ameriki, an' if I don' live there, I see 'em from the train." He had learned to speak English in his soft way, studied to become a citizen, and sent his sisters fat envelopes filled with money and news of life in America. Not only did this money support them, it also provided each with a generous dowry – the guarantee, it was thought, of a good marriage. It was his duty to do this as the only male left in the family.

He worked so hard for his sisters, he had no money to provide for a wife and family of his own, and lived his entire life as a bachelor. Then, after forty-nine years in the United States, he retired and returned with his American passport and Social Security checks to his homeland and to the island of his childhood.

He lived in the old family home with his only surviving sister, Eviania. Two or three mornings a week after matins, he climbed the hill above the town and slowly made his way out to the vineyard in the country. Rooted near the moss-grown wall sprouted the tiny one-room farmhouse he was born in. Sheltered from the noon sun, he sometimes had a lunch of cheese, bread and tomatoes followed by a nap, waiting out the heat of the day. Later, he carefully tended the grapes and other fruit, harvesting what was ripe to take back to town. Sometimes he paid a visit to Anna.

I had heard his story often in the two years I knew him. I'd ask him how he felt about his life, about all the sacrifices he had made. And he always answered, "I'm satisfied."

Across the fields the sun's rays had ignited the wheat in white flame, and the entire landscape was etched into a relief of brilliant light here, deep lengthening shadows there. He reached for his cane. Out on the terrace, I thanked him for the gifts from his garden. "From God," he said, pointing his finger to the sky. He was eighty-two and not quite five feet tall.

"Could I have a little kiss?" he looked at me shyly. "It would mean so much to me."

It was the first time he had ever asked me for such a sign of affection. I smiled, reached down and took his face in my two hands, touching a kiss on his cheek.

"Goodbye, Anna." He turned, smiling, and left.

"Goodbye, Yiorgos." I said in Greek, and then the traditional phrase for leavetakings, "*Pás stó kaló.*" Go with the good.

*   *   *

One day, about a week later, I washed my laundry in two big buckets on the terrace and spent the rest of the day painting and reading. About six o'clock I decided to make a late trip to town to check the mail. It was Saturday, the last chance to mail a letter to a friend in the States. I decided not to change out of my jeans and wrinkled blouse, because it was just going to be a quick trip, twenty minutes down the hill, five minutes in the post and twenty minutes up again. I wanted to have a quiet evening.

Entering the town I passed Yiorgos's house as usual on my way to the post office. I was first aware of the lights on in the parlor, lights that were never on, seen through a door that was never open. Parlors are rarely used – only for holidays, wedding feasts. . . . On the narrow portico, propped to the right of the open door was the familiar blue coffin cover. As the white-bearded priest stepped carefully around it and descended the steps to the street, I stopped him.

"Papá, who has died?"

"Yiorgos," he answered. "He collapsed at vespers, and they carried him home in a chair. He died two hours ago."

I entered the parlor and there was the blue casket, resting on two straight-backed chairs to which someone had attached fat beeswax candles, one at the head and the other at the foot. What everyone had agreed was Yiorgos – and which, in my shock, I couldn't seem to believe – was there, in the casket, covered by a blanket of chrysan-themums and sweet basil. His nieces and nephews, his one surviving sister, were seated around him moaning "Uncle! Aiyee, Uncle!!" His sister wailed messages for him to relay to their mother and father. "Tell them I'll be following soon; we'll all be together soon!" At the setting of the sun they covered his face with a vinegar-soaked handkerchief. The ritual of the wake had begun.

Yes, he was there, in that box, the air strangely vibrating above him. In the pit of my stomach I felt the unreality of seeing him there, face hidden, and so still.

I looked up, and above the large antique buffet hung a life-sized photograph of a young man of about twenty with dark hair and gentle eyes. The full head of hair confused me until I realized that yes, it was Yiorgos. He had probably bought that photograph with the first real paycheck he could call his own. The thought lanced the protective bubble of my shock, and I relived his life as he told it, remembering his untimely, timely visits, his gifts – his peace.

The wailing stopped for a moment. "Look!" I heard the whisper echoed round the room, "She cries . . . Anna cries."

Chapter Three
Iraklis

"Though in many of its aspects
this visible world seems formed in love,
the invisible spheres were formed in fright."
– Herman Melville

WHAT FOLLOWS IS THE STORY MY FRIEND IRAKLIS TOLD me the first time I met him in 1973. He was sitting in a cafe, deep in animated conversation with an American friend of mine who lived on the island. Karolina spotted me passing by among the bronzed tourists and vegetable-laden donkeys and called me over to meet him. We should have a lot in common, she said. Iraklis was a painter too.

He was a short muscular man, about fifty-five or sixty, dressed in an immaculate, sun-faded shirt with rolled-up sleeves, and a pair of army drab trousers. His bright blue eyes and rosy tan set off the white fringe of hair emerging under a blue canvas hat. This hat shaded his bald head as well as a prominant nose that dove out over his nearly toothless smile as he helped me in Greek to pronounce his unusual name.

* * *

I am very pleased to meet you. But, it is Iraklis. No, not HER- cules, Ee-ra-KLEES. That's right. Ah, you want to know how I came to live on Mykonos? Well, it is an interesting story — an adventure, in fact.

At the time, I was living in Mytilini, on the Island of Lesbos. I was born there, and I still have a brother who lives there with his wife and daughter. Except for my brother and a few cousins, I have no other family.

Well. You know about the miraculous icon of the Blessed Virgin on Tinos, that island there? I had always wanted to visit it. It is only a half-hour boat ride from here, but it takes two days from Mytilini. This was in 1965, and I was nearing my fiftieth year and had never visited her shrine on Tinos. You see, Greeks feel they must go there at least once in their lifetime. There is another shrine like it, I think, in France; you've probably heard of it, yes? Where the Virgin heals many sick people? The same thing at Tinos. But I wasn't sick; I am never sick, or at least not seriously, so there never seemed to be a reason to go. But because I was getting older, I thought it was time to pay her a visit, and I decided to go on her biggest feastday, the Assumption, on August fifteenth.

I didn't want to sail on the commercial boats. I don't like crowds, and all the ships would be overflowing with pilgrims heading for Tinos. I had a small sailboat, about three meters long, that I had been fixing up. It had a single triangular sail, but I had fitted it out for rowing too, so I could take it around the coast of Lesbos for octopus. The idea came to me that I would take this boat, and I set about getting it ready.

As the day approached, I became very excited at the prospect of sailing into Tinos harbor in this little boat. I could just see the looks of surprise on the faces of those who would be on the pier when I arrived. "Where are you from?" they would call as I neared the mooring. "I am Iraklis, from Mytilini!"

My brother and his family tried to talk me out of sailing alone, but I was determined to go ahead as planned. We are very different, my brother and I. He has never understood why I didn't live a "good" life: buy a house, settle down with a wife, have children and work at a job that brought in lots of money. The house I could agree with; we need shelter. But all the rest, he could have it; that life was not for me. No one from the family was at the harbor when I left. They didn't want me to go alone by sailboat, so they didn't show up to say good-bye; that's just the way they are. So, there was no one on the pier to cast me off and to wish me "Kaló Taxídi" but Lazarus, who had been drinking all night and happened to pass by on his way home.

The first day out was beautiful, with just enough breeze to keep up an easy pace. I ate, had a little sleep, read or watched for dolphins. I was making good time and expected to arrive in Tinos early the next afternoon. That first day it seemed the Virgin herself smiled on me and blessed my passage.

But as the fates would have it, the next morning I woke up becalmed. The sea was thick as honey, and it was clear I would have to row for a while. I lowered the sail and brought out the oars. I was sure the breeze would rise any moment, yet it didn't feel right just to sit and wait for it. And so I rowed. By early afternoon, the time I had expected to arrive, I was in the middle of an empty and silent sea, where the few distant islands I could identify from the map seemed to float above its surface as if suspended on platforms of mist. You have probably seen such days from land; you should experience one sometime from the sea! The water itself seemed to be sweating.

I rowed, drank some water and rowed some more. It was clear by two that the breeze would not pick up, and so I stopped and ate some olives and cheese under the canopy I had made out of the sail. Then I dozed and rowed again. Progress was slow, as you can imagine. But there was no point in turning back. I was strong, and I rowed on. Even at nightfall, when the usual breeze failed to come, I rowed on — and through the night too, I rowed, falling asleep finally around three, praying for just a breath of a breeze.

But when I woke at dawn the third day out, my eyes opened to the same silent water, the same mute sail.

You are right, I am strong. I keep fit by not eating meat, and I do calisthenics every day. But after fifteen hours of rowing, I was reaching the limit of my endurance. Or so I thought. The heat was making my mind play tricks, and as the third day wore on, I began to see mirages of the harbor at Tinos and the white village with the great Shrine at its center. I hoped the Virgin would give me strength to go on. A few hours later another mirage appeared, like two smudges on the horizon. I kept rowing. After half an hour or so I looked again. They were still there, and bigger yet. A quick check of the map showed it was not a mirage, but the twin headlands of Tinos and Mykonos far off in the distance. Suddenly the windvane at the top of the mast started to spin, and the canopy luffed down gently, then immediately snapped up again with a loud retort. I rushed to raise the sail and set the course, revived by the freshness of the breeze and the knowledge that I was so close to my destination.

But, you know, it was August, and the Meltemi in this part of the Aegean is a treacherous wind. It can blow and blow for days without letting up; and then it just stops, and there will be no wind for a day or two. Suddenly, just as you are getting used to the calm, it blows up again. I was from Mytilini, and though I knew of the Meltemi, I had never experienced it sailing in a small boat. The idea that my trip might coincide with it never once occurred to me.

So one minute all was silent and becalmed and, within a half hour, my world had turned topsy-turvy, like a loukomáda (a doughnut-like sweet) in boiling oil. Because of the violence of the wind I had to lower the sail to almost nothing. I hung onto the tiller with great difficulty, trying to tack toward Tinos. But it was no use; instead I found myself foundering toward the jagged rocks off the northern tip of Mykonos! Somehow, by the intercession of the Virgin, I'm sure, I was able to slowly guide the boat away from the rocks and head toward a deep bay I had noted on the map.

The mouth of the bay was guarded by several small islets and because of this, the currents in the region were unpredictable and caused the waves to collide with one another, sending up spumes of water twenty feet into the air. It was a sobering sight you can be sure, and yet, I had to get past it, out of the currents and into the bay, where I was certain I would find a haven. Unfortunately, just when I was almost through the channel between two islets, a big swell raised the boat up high, where it was caught by another swell coming from the opposite direction. Both the boat and I flipped like toys and fell into the wild sea.

Another few seconds under those waves and I'm sure my last gasp would have taken in a liter of seawater. By the time I surfaced, I was well clear of the rocks and, thanks be to God, spotted the wreckage of the boat off to my right. Though the wind was still high, the sea appeared less tur-bulent in the bay, so I was able to reach the wreckage, part of the keel, with little trouble. I clung to it and drifted with the waves slowly like that as the sun set and it got dark. I had little concept of time, but it seemed as if I drifted for hours, and I even must have dozed off. Somehow, I never lost my grip on the wreckage. The next thing I knew, the sky was beginning to lighten, and I heard waves crashing on what sounded like a sandy shore. When my feet touched bottom, all thought left me except to get to the beach, where I collapsed and slept like a dead man. This was where Andreaus found me a few hours later.

He was just a youngster then, eleven or twelve years old. He was down on the beach looking for salvage that had blown in during the storm. He found me! My bald head had shone like gold in the sunlight, he told me, and had caught his attention. Andreaus tried to get me to come up to the house where his mother would give me food and a bed to sleep in. But I am very independent and said no, that I was strong and was all right as I was. He persisted, though, and as my mind cleared, I had to admit I was hungry — and very thirsty.

On the long hike up the trail from the beach I tried to determine how *long I had been in the water. I remembered capsizing and later watching the sun go down as I clung to the keel. The capsize would have occurred at about four o'clock. When I landed on the beach I remembered the sky was just beginning to lighten, which in Mytilini occurs around five at that time of year. So it took me from four in the afternoon until roughly five the next morning to drift in to shore. I had been in the water thirteen hours.*

While I ate breakfast I told Andreaus and his mother, Eleni, about the last three days. Then they gave me a bed up on the balcony off the main room, and I slept until Andreaus's father came home late in the afternoon. We all had a coffee together as I told Vassilis the story of how I came to be sitting in his parlor. Vassilis was a morose, dark sort of man, due perhaps to his suffering from a chronic sickness in his spleen. He just died a few years ago, in fact. But up until then, he worked whenever he could on construction to bring in some extra money. Andreaus had left school that year and would soon go to Athens to learn a trade.

Vassilis and the boy took me outside and showed me the farm. They had twenty-four sheep, six goats and three donkeys, a few fields surrounding the house and one to the north for pasturing. Near the edge of their land, Vassilis's grandfather had built the family chapel. Just over the wall from the chapel, at the edge of a field they rented, Vassilis pointed out a small barn. It was almost falling to ruin, but if I liked, he said, I could live there rent free for as long as I wanted.

Well, I thought about Mytilini and the differences between my brother and me. I thought about how peaceful it was here, far from the crush of Mytilini, which is a large city, the capital of the Dodacanese. So I wrote my family that I was accepting Vassilis's generous offer to stay in this small shelter — maybe for a few months or, at the most, a year. I would make a proper door, put in a window or two, and it would be quite comfortable. And this is what I did, except that instead of six months or a year, I have stayed eight, almost nine years now . . .

*   *   *

Since Iraklis had arrived so dramatically that day in August almost nine years before, his life had settled into a simple routine. He lived quietly, making a modest living painting signs and keeping records of the truckloads of sand taken from the beach for construction. In his free time he read — mostly religious books and the Bible, for he was, I learned with time, a kind of lay monk. He also had begun to paint. At his invitation, I paid him the first of many visits for lunch, visits that all followed more or less the same routine.

The first item of business on arrival was the viewing of his paintings. He unrolled canvases depicting village scenes and landscapes where the paint had been brushed on directly from the tubes in raw, unmixed colors. It was obvious great attention had been paid, in true primitive style, to the careful rendering of each individual stone, every blade of grass. Next he brought out the portraits, done from old photographs, more sophisticated than the landscapes in their color rendering, but betraying still the primitive's endless quest for the perfect likeness. Then last, and somewhat sheepishly, he unrolled paintings of young, beautiful women, one or two of them idealized in prim dresses or, to my restrained delight, undressed, smiling head-to-waist portraits with glistening red lips and full, round breasts, capped with marvelously pink, taut nipples. He sort of flashed these paintings before my amused gaze and then hastily rolled them up again. I praised them all, lavishly.

With the paintings again packed and out of the way, he moved a crude table between two benches, covered it with newspaper and brought on the meal. Usually he served white beans cooked in a blackened pot over a wood fire. We smothered these beans in olive oil and raw onions and, combined with the taste of woodsmoke, such a delicacy was created from this homely fare that I would invariably eat two or three platefuls and suffer for the next week. To accompany the beans he'd make a green salad, and we speared our forks into the common plate of shredded lettuce sprinkled with fresh dill, lemon juice and oil. Then with two glasses of steaming tea before us and some sweet biscuits for dessert, Iraklis began his stories.

When they speak, Greeks are normally very demonstrative in their body language. But I think that for my benefit, since my knowledge of Greek was rudimentary at that point, Iraklis felt compelled to punctuate his stories with even more graphic pantomime than usual. He boasted a little about what a good influence he had been on Andreaus, the young boy who had found him on the beach (and whom I would meet later and consider marrying). He had taught Andreaus calisthenics (here Iraklis extended his arms above his head and retracted them several times) as a substitute for other activities that seemed to preoccupy adolescent boys and which he didn't pantomime, but called "working alone with the little bird."

Prior to all this good influence from Iraklis, Andreaus was not only on the road to perdition, but was unhealthy as well: because the family was so poor, he sometimes had to go without shoes even in winter, so he always seemed to be fighting a cold. At this point, Iraklis drew his thumb and forefinger down the length of his generous nose, pinched off the imaginary gob and flicked it to the ground, not forgetting, with the primitive's attention to detail, to wipe the residue off on his pants. And whenever he spoke of them, which was often, he illustrated the Greek word for "woman" by drawing his two closed fists up to his chest.

But his most extraordinary tales, the ones that seemed to have had the greatest impact on his life and, I should add, the ones that brought to full flower his talent for mime, were the stories of the times he had come close to death.

He'd always had a strong sense of adventure. And he liked to trace it back to his earliest childhood when, as a three-year-old, he climbed up the back of a chair in the family apartment to look through a window where dust particles, sparkling in the rays of the noonday sun streaming down the light shaft, had attracted his attention. As he brought his legs up onto the sill, he lost his balance and fell several stories to the bottom of the shaft, where he remained, bruised but miraculously alive, until the downstairs neighbor returning from work for her siesta heard his cries.

Another time, when he was twelve, he heard a freighter toot in the harbor miles away and, right then, decided to seek his fortune wherever it might lead. He had no money for a bus, so he caught a ride on the back of a car. He slipped off when the car took a sharp turn, and his belt buckle hooked on the bumper. He was dragged several yards before he finally detached himself and skidded to a stop. With limbs all skinned and bloody, he finally reached the harbor and sneaked on board one of the freighters lined up along the pier. But before he could find a suitable place in which to stow himself, he was caught by an unsympathetic sailor and escorted home.

And, of course, there was that story of his incredible sea voyage in a ten-foot sailboat and being cast away, soggy and exhausted, onto one of the pristine beaches of Mykonos. But for Iraklis it was war that held the life-changing experiences, where priorities were tested involving the primal issue of survival.

Iraklis was approaching the age for enlistment into the Greek army, and by the time he was called, Mussolini had plans for invading Greece from the north through Albania. Iraklis found himself dangling on the horns of an age-old dilemma: could he kill or not? What planted the seed of his conflict occurred a year or two earlier when he had begun to read the Bible, drawn to it more out of curiosity than out of any conscious spiritual need. Here again, the old injunctions loomed before him, this time with new and immediate meaning: "Thou shalt not kill. . . . He who kills by the sword shall die by the sword." But as a soldier he was expected to kill, and if he didn't, at least in self-defense, the prospect of his own annihilation seemed inevitable.

Perhaps if he approached the problem from a different angle: *who* was he killing, then? That much seemed clear enough: young men like himself, with dreams of living full, active lives, young men who just happened to come from another country, who might believe in what they were doing – or who might be groping for answers as he was. It was true; he had no quarrel with these young Italian soldiers as individuals. Yet Italy, the nation, was about to invade his homeland, and it was his duty to defend it. But to do so, he must kill. On the other hand, to defend his peace of mind, he must *not* kill. To whom did the greater duty lie then: to Greece, or to God?

As his resolution swung first to one choice and then to the other, memories of having been spared certain death in the past began to flood his mind, and an invitation to trust began to emerge from the chaos of "shalt"s and "shalt not"s. Soon he saw himself no longer dangling between the horns of a dilemma, but squirming like a fish on the end of a hook, eyeball to eyeball with the fisherman. There would be no guarantees. It must be a leap of faith and nothing less; he must be prepared to die for the stand he was about to take.

After basic training, Iraklis was sent to Albania. One day a company of Italian soldiers swept down on his camp from the surrounding hills. Iraklis recognized the moment and, before fear of dying could change his mind, he hastily removed the bullets from his rifle and scattered them, and all his extra ammunition, on the ground before him. If there was fear at that point, it was fear of going back on his vow more than anything else. When he had finished, he stood where he was, eyes closed, and quietly prepared to die.

The Italians poured over the camp like a flash flood. They ran by Iraklis on his left and on his right as both Italians and Greeks fell dead or wounded. They kept coming and coming until suddenly it was all over. And, as the silence of the dead faded before the moaning of those wounded, Iraklis found to his utter amazement that he was alive. Nothing had touched him. As he bent to help the injured, he wondered how this could be so. It was as if, in the heat and chaos of battle, the Italians hadn't even seen him – as if he had been invisible.

I wondered about this, about how many other Greeks might have died because Iraklis failed to defend himself – and them. But not until later. In the moments after I heard this story I just sat in amazement. To voluntarily give up your life for a principle. I had often asked myself if I could do something like that. I doubted it. And most of the people I knew couldn't have done it either. Not that we were bad people, or even weak people, but that the drive for survival was simply so strong and compelling; to block out the survival instinct would take tremendous strength – or tremendous faith. Granting even that, our own indomitable pride might have prevented our becoming, as Iraklis would soon become in the eyes of some, a fool. God's fool, perhaps.

To Iraklis it was a miracle: once again he had been given life when circumstances had dictated certain death. A wave of humility and gratitude swept over him for the deliverance granted by a suddenly very personal God. He must dedicate his life to this God; he must build an altar, present a thank offering before the Throne.

But what could he possibly give? The gift of life was priceless. It seemed clear, then, that he must give up some of its greatest pleasures: for one, he would stop eating meat. Never again would he enjoy succulent pork or lamb roasted for hours over hot coals. He would give up liquor, though he never drank much, and with it the male camaraderie in the *tavernas*. But he had always had an inclination for solitude anyway, so this wouldn't be much to give up either. What could he give that would be a true sacrifice?

For a Greek man there was only one thing that was valued more than anything – even more than his life – and that was his family. It was settled then; he would become celibate. He would never come home as other men, to his woman, his children, and experience the joy of family, warm hearth and bed. For Iraklis there would be no heirs. Most men would rather die than give up such things; many die in wars to preserve them. But Iraklis had experienced the touch of God, and he knew he was no longer the same as before – no longer the same as other men.

It was clear these new vows would be difficult to sustain, for he was in the world, after all, and not in a monastery. He would have to redouble his efforts to discipline his body through calisthenics and his mind through reading and prayer.

"Other men read books about sex and violence," he told me once, "but I read the Bible. I have read it four or five times now. See, here I am at *Lukianós*," opening his worn volume to Luke. "Whenever I get tired, I lie down and read a while, sleep a little and then read some more. I read other books too, mostly the lives of the saints and books like that, but when I read the Bible, I fly."

*   *   *

Then it was July 1982, and I was on the Island of Lesbos, creaking
down a winding road in a decrepit Mercedes bus, seeking the home
of my friend, Iraklis, whom I hadn't seen since he had left Mykonos
for good a year and a half before. He and I had a lot to talk about;
we might not see each other for a long time.

The driver let me off at the sign for his village, and I approached
the cafe to ask directions. The dry air shimmered in the midday heat.
A gray-uniformed policeman was seated at a table, and I asked him
if he knew the way to Iraklis's house.

"The painter?" he asked. "It's back in the direction you came from."
He tipped back his coffee cup, draining it. "I'll take you there. He's
a friend of mine."

After about half a kilometer, he guided his motorbike off the main
road onto a dirt one. We bounced along in the ruts for about three
blocks and turned left again onto a narrow dirt path, past a small house,
and then took a right onto a footpath barely visible through the sparse
grasses of the fallow field. Finally, we pulled up to a weathered red gate.
Beyond it, out of the small white house with green trim, came Iraklis.

"Ha! Do you believe it?!" I shouted in Greek, laughing. "Did you
get my card?"

He smiled, yes, and welcome, and gave me a hug. "That's your house,"
he pointed to the tiny one with a peaked roof near the one he came out
of. "Let me put your pack inside." He was not used to company and
chattered on from one subject to another. I thanked the policeman,
who was preparing to leave, declining Iraklis's offer of a coffee. As the
policeman revved up his engine, Iraklis turned and swept his arm in
a wide semicircle, announcing with a broad, toothless smile, "My home!"

There was an acre of land and two tiny houses set around a small terrace. He never used the smaller house, he said, except for storage and for
an occasional guest. Near the door of the larger house, a cement table
tilted at a slight angle on the stump of an old olive tree. Inside, I saw a
room measuring about seven by fourteen feet, and this one room served
as his kitchen, living room and bedroom. Another crude cement table
supported a three-burner stove connected by a rubber hose to a metal
cylinder of butane gas. To the left of the door was an enormous clay
amphora for his supply of olive oil, which he dipped out with the battered metal measuring cup hanging by wire from a hook above. There
were two windows, a round wrought-iron table, a director's chair and a
narrow iron bed, painted white and covered with an old, but clean

looking army blanket. On another table under the front window, he kept two kerosene lamps, a cassette player and a small pile of books. A dime-store picture of Jesus praying at Gethsemane was nailed over the bed. It was a simple, utilitarian shelter with no aesthetic relief.

"Other men live in big houses and have a car and spend all their money on gasoline and decorating their homes," he boasted, "but not me. I'm happy living here. I have everything I need and plenty of time to read when I want."

Outside again, I noticed that water from the rinsed dishes drained easily from the cement table and quenched a thirsty squash plant just beginning to climb a string to an arbor over the terrace. We began a tour of his acre, heading first for the vegetable garden.

As we rounded the corner of the house, I was startled by the sudden appearance of a woman in a blue shirt and black slacks. Her head crowned in a tousled orange wig, she stood looking off in the distance, one foot primly placed slightly ahead of the other: Iraklis's latest artistic achievement, the scarecrow Amalia, who during my brief visit, caused me to do a number of double takes every time she crept into my peripheral vision.

The garden was beginning to yield the first fruits of spring planting. Tomatoes had just begun to blush and one or two large ones seemed ripe enough to pick. The eggplants, too, hid like deep maroon presences brooding among the light green leaves. Beans climbed a makeshift trellis and zucchini mounds with huge leaves sheltered the young squash from the sun. I saw rows of garlic, and onions with their tightly packed flowers swaying heavily in the light breeze. The ground was poor – basically sandy, red clay – better for making bricks, I thought, than for sprouting vegetables. Yet his little garden appeared to do well, to flourish, in fact, in the inhospitable soil. I shared this observation with him.

"Other men spray their gardens with all kinds of chemicals, but not me," he answered. "There's not one bit of poison on those eggplants," he pointed to the healthy plants. "See how unblemished the tomatoes and zucchini are? You will see later just how sweet they taste. Other men use chemicals and treat their soil with fertiizers, but not me. You know why? Because I have faith!"

I was impressed – and delighted by his unabashed bragging.

We moved on to scout the perimeter of his land, which was secured by a sturdy chickenwire fence. This was olive country. As with all the small garden farms in this area, his houses crouched right in among the trees of an immense olive grove that covered a valley below a ring of high hills. The olive grove was crisscrossed by a network of dirt roads and paths leading to small summer communities of huts like his own. People from the hill villages came down to the valley, spending summers near their gardens, and then moved up to the villages again for the winter. Because he enjoyed solitude, Iraklis was the only one who lived in the valley year round.

Back at the house, he made me sit in the shade while he prepared a lunch of potatoes and eggplant fried in olive oil. He had picked the two ripe tomatoes for our salad – the simple tomato and onion salad of summer, for there would be no lettuce in this arid season until October. It was a lunch of first fruits "in honor of your visit," he announced, and we gave thanks as he crossed himself. Moved by the warmth of his welcome, I surrendered to the uncharacteristic urge to do likewise.

After lunch I went to my little house for a nap. It was a third the size of Iraklis's, and allowed room for only an old iron bed and an unused wooden icebox alongside. There was a narrow walkway between the wall and the bed, and a wooden box piled high with blankets took up the few inches at its foot. Draped on their lower halves with swatches of an old lace tablecloth, two small windows faced each other from opposite walls like defiant belly dancers. Iraklis had painted the peaked, corrugated tin ceiling a bright cerulean blue – "like the sky," he had said when he brought in my pack. But the roof provided shelter from only direct rays of the sun; the heat inside and out remained oppressive.

Nevertheless, the light, that famous Greek light, permeated the room with a soft iridescence, where even the shadows revealed their inherent detail, and everything that had form was set off in sharp relief. I crawled between clean white sheets, my eyes resting on the six-inch shard of mirror propped up on the narrow ledge near the window opposite me.

It had been a long trip, and I slept dreamlessly for a couple hours. The sun was lower when I woke, and the heat had lost its intensity. The entire landscape seemed refreshed and relaxed. Iraklis made coffee to drink out of his tiny stoneware cups. There were hours to go before dinner, so he proposed a walk down to the sea.

We passed other houses like Iraklis's and at a few he greeted the farmers who sat near their doorways sipping coffee, passing the time before they had to water their gardens.

The sea filled a deeply-hewn gulf that probed far into this part of the island. Lowering steadily, the sun, had lit its waters into a golden cauldron. The shore wasn't sandy, but dark and rocky; always the beachcomber, I noticed there were no pretty stones. All of them were darkened, in fact, like river stones near cities. The gulf was polluted, Iraklis explained. It was forbidden to swim or to sell fish from its waters. Beautiful to look at, but not to touch.

Ten years ago a private company built a shoe factory near the mouth where it bottlenecked into a narrow channel leading out to the open Aegean. All the factory waste was trapped in the gulf, essentially an inland salt lake. People relaxed in cafes and restaurants that lined the shore, enjoying the beauty of the changing light. But no one could take a swim that hot day, or enjoy grilled fish taken from those waters. The natural enjoyment of life, so prevalent in Greek society, seemed muted here, subdued and sterile. There were, in fact, few children in evidence.

And there were no foreigners, I noticed, and few women, for no one but men normally inhabited the cafes at this hour on a weekday. Iraklis wanted to stop in one of them and have an orange soda. Then we moved on to another, and he insisted on stopping there, so we ordered coffee. As we entered each cafe all heads turned, and conversation stopped; the men sat, secure in their element, watching us in unveiled curiosity, the soccer match on the TV forgotten. Iraklis was apparently known for his celibacy, and now he was seen with a foreign woman.

I was beginning to get the picture. He was caught in the dilemma of wanting to show me off and, at the same time, needing to defend my virtue and his own.

"*Pós pái?*" (Indeed, how *was* it going, I was beginning to wonder), the inevitable question was raised, as among perpetual schoolboys everywhere.

Iraklis launched off in short rapid sentences that were greeted with polite, though slightly knowing smiles, as if to believe him in the presence of their cronies put their own manhood at stake.

"No," Iraklis protested. "She's an American." He didn't introduce me. "She lives on Mykonos. I have known her for fifteen years," he exaggerated. "She speaks Greek."

I squirmed in my seat and looked directly at them, feeling mean, fighting both the urge to say something and the heat that glowed crimson as a fever that I could feel rising in my cheeks. Walking back later, I cleared my throat and mentioned all the attention we were getting.

"To them," he said, "seeing you was like seeing a comet." I burst out laughing at this, my anger dissolving fast, as he launched into another "apologia," apparently in need of his own solace.

"After all," he said, "other men go after women and drink and waste their lives, but I gave up women and don't drink or eat meat — rarely even an egg. All those animal products are like dynamite. Even so," he added with a shrug, "every night my birdie rises like the moon, and I can't do a thing about it."

It was already dark when we arrived home, almost too tired to eat. But we did anyway, settling for a snack of cheese and bread, a few olives, washed down with water. Iraklis gave me one of his two kerosene lamps to light the way to my room.

The orange glow of the lamplight had turned the bright cerulean ceiling into a soft gray, and all the corners and covered things illuminated six hours before had sunk into deep, inarticulate shadow. I took out my journal, and in the dim light tried to record the day, barely able to think, because of the blanket of weariness settling over me. Finally, I gave up fighting both fatigue and bad light and relaxed into the sheets, musing on the significance of artificial light as it compared with the power of natural sunlight, where even the corners and covered things were revealed, where even the shadows held form and meaning within them.

The next morning Iraklis boiled tea, which we dipped dry rusks into, accompanied by a crumbly white country cheese. And a neighbor had left thick, creamy sheep's milk the night before while we were on our walk. After breakfast I caught the bus to town where I shopped for fish and coffee and arranged to fly back to Mykonos the next day.

When I returned at noon, I was surprised to see a woman sitting on the terrace. She gazed at me with dull eyes as I approached and didn't smile when Iraklis introduced us. I wondered if she were retarded. This was Meltiades' wife, Maria – the Meltiades, Iraklis explained, who had left the fresh sheep's milk as a gift of welcome to his guest; Meltiades, Iraklis added in private, who regularly beat his epileptic wife and who stole her government subsidy to buy whiskey. Kind, thoughtful Meltiades was a wife batterer; numb and dull-eyed Maria, who sat before us, was his victim.

There was a scar on her forehead and a bruise as big as a pancake on her thigh, which she revealed, raising the hem of her black skirt. A fresh red scrape on her calf smarted still from skidding in the dirt when he hit her the night before. And there was an enormous star etched into her left arm, which, she explained in the same deadpan voice, was not caused by her husband, but by a nasty wasp bite when she was a child. And we commiserated, saying "Oh!" and "How horrible that must have been" and "Yes, to have made such a huge scar!"

Why the unease we felt at the immediacy of the fresh wound, the close proximity of violence? Why our strange relief in deflecting attention to a scar of the past, visited on innocence by a fluke of nature? Later that day I thought about these questions.

Iraklis unwrapped the fish. I had asked the advice of the fishmonger in town as to what would make the best soup. He pointed out the medium-sized sea bass and the large pink flying fish with oversized fins and enormous blue eyes. Iraklis nodded in approval. He scaled the flying fish first, slitting open its belly and pulling out the entrails. Then he hooked his forefinger under the loop of gills and ripped them out, explaining they would give the soup a bitter taste. The bass was cleaned, and he washed both fish in cold water until they gleamed bright-eyed and fresh on the stoneware platter.

Maria sat quietly with sad eyes, sipping coffee and watching everything we did. She was afraid to go home, she had said, where he lay in his heavy midday slumber. Iraklis tried to make light of it, to get her to laugh, but I felt her lonely sorrow seep into and prod the marrow of my own memory, and I told him no, how I understood; you have to be a woman to understand, Iraklis, to know it's not a laughing matter, cannot be joked about, Iraklis.

The soup was done; its fragrance filled the small house and wafted outside to the whitewashed terrace where the sun glared in full, blinding intensity. It was too hot to eat there and we moved into his small room, arranging the round wrought-iron table in the center. Maria and I sat on the bed. Before he drew up the director's chair, Iraklis ladled steaming broth into large soup plates and set the platter of fish in the center. He brought lemon quarters, thick slices of bread and a salad of tomato wedges and green onions in their dressing of olive oil from his own trees. There were small gray-green olives and glasses of *retzina* (Iraklis had a token glass with us), which we clinked together, drinking to each other's good health.

Maria sat primly on the bed beside me, white paper napkin in her lap, bread in left hand, eating slowly and daintily with her right, back straight, as if she had just graduated from an English finishing school. We took our time, relishing the soup, a soothing broth laced with lemon juice, and the white, flaky meat of the fish, fresh smelling and firm. Iraklis noisily sucked the bones of the heads, locating the fish's cheeks tucked into the skull, delicacies like oysters in mother-of-pearl.

But there could be no more delaying. She must go now, she said, as she put her napkin on the table. And no, she didn't want to put us to the trouble of finding her a bed for a siesta, and we must sleep; the hot sun and full stomachs have made us drowsy. Maria wasn't sleepy, though. She could not afford the luxury of relaxing into pleasant dreams. She must return, dull-eyed and inert, to her personal, unending nightmare. I sought some word of comfort, some sense of hope, but I found nothing.

"Can you pray?" I asked, lamely. Blank-faced, she turned slowly in the direction of her house.

"I have no heart," she said.

Iraklis and I cleaned up the mess from the meal and left the dishes to drain on the terrace table. We didn't say much; we were both deep in our thoughts. Suddenly he blurted out that it was the first time she had come like that. Whatever happened must have been very bad.

"Could it be because I am here?" I ventured my suspicions, recalling our experience in the cafes the night before. I was an unattached and unchaperoned foreign woman, a rare and apparently provocative phenomenon in this small village.

"No, I don't think so," Iraklis tried to reassure me. "He has been beating her for years."

It was good that I would be leaving tomorrow, I thought, remembering Maria's somber greeting when we were introduced, her furtive eyes as we prepared lunch.

Iraklis shook his head and tried to divert my attention. "But," he said, almost as if this should explain the whole matter, "She never takes a bath!"

"Never? Not even once a week, for Sunday?"

"Not once a month! She's a real country woman, like in the old days. And you know," he seemed compelled to add, "she did a very bad thing once. She went to the police and told them her husband drank and beat her and spent the money on whiskey that the government sent for her disability. The police couldn't do anything and sent her away. It was a very bad thing for her do do. She has a father up in the village; why didn't she go to him? She's not a good woman, really. How a person can never take a bath, I can't understand it."

And I thought of Maria eating.

I went to my room to lie down, immediately plunging into a fitful sleep punctuated by a tangle of dreams. After a couple hours I drifted awake, feeling chilled. The bright sunlight on the terrace had faded, and the light had assumed a green cast. I sensed more than actually saw that it was getting darker. From the doorway I could see a huge bank of dark clouds boiling down on us from the hills ringing the valley. A distant swishing sound was getting louder and louder as the north wind flicked up every silver-green leaf on each olive tree as it swept down the hill. Our own trees below remained still, and the cicadas chimed on their cacophonous jeer, invisible and incessant. Suddenly, one of the plastic plates drying in the stack on the cement table rose up, tipped and sailed ten feet like a frisbee before careening to the ground. Then the air was full of plates and pots crashing and clanging all over the terrace floor, as if some invisible hand had come down and swept the table clean. It began to rain.

The unseasonable storm cooled everything. When the sun broke through again, I felt exhilarated, as on the first crisp fall day, only this was July, and two hours ago it had been a hundred in the shade. We put on sweaters and went about getting dinner. I poured *ouzos* into thimble-sized glasses and passed a *mezé* of tiny olives and chunks of goat's cheese. Iraklis once again waived his drinking vow in honor of the renewal of good feeling, and we clinked glasses to each other's health.

We heard the peaceful music of tinkling bells, and in the distance, beyond the vegetable garden and another field, two figures approached. It was Meltiades and Maria passing by, Iraklis announced, taking their small flock to pasture for the night, as they did every evening after milking.

Suddenly the golden light of the sun setting over the rain-washed hills was shattered, and a strangely familiar gauze curtain seemed to fall before the scene as the screams filled the air. Only they weren't screams; they were harsh, crude cries, like some animal, high-pitched and sharp. And the blows, brisk thwacks, loud as from a flat piece of wood. He had her by one arm, hitting her with the wood, and they danced their lurching circles until at last he flung her to the ground and stamped off, driving the startled sheep up into the night pasture. Maria ran limping into the trees, and then there was nothing but silence and the diminishing echo of retreating bells.

We stood as if struck into marble, as unmoving and uncomprehending as the scarecrow Amalia, I holding the plate of olives and cheese, Iraklis with a knife in one hand and a half-peeled potato in the other. We had stood silent in our strange attitudes throughout the beating, never moving, never calling out, never interfering.

"Why didn't we do something?!" I cried at Iraklis. "How could we have just stood here? All I had to do was call out, and that might have stopped it."

*   *   *

I remembered the summer and autumn two years before when fear took me for a joyride to the nether reaches of my experience thus far. It came disguised in the form of a young biker from northern England and lay dormant, waiting out the glow of our growing infatuation.

We met through a mutual friend, a distinguished gallery owner and educator from Dorset County, England.

"I've got a friend I'd like a portrait of," Lawrence had said. "Would you paint it? He's coming in a fortnight."

I promised to give it a try. But the person who sat in my living room two weeks later was going to present quite a challenge. Eyes downcast in shame or self-hatred, straight hair, long and sticking out at all angles, beer belly, this young man was clearly in trouble with himself. Many weeks later, Lawrence revealed to me the secret of Larry's drug and alcohol addiction.

"Would you like me to do your portrait?" I asked.

"If you want to," he looked at me for the first time, seemingly without a will of his own.

His name was Larry, Lawrence and Larry, the one an appendage of the other. Larry came to sit three or four times. As I worked, we talked about his childhood in Leeds; his experience at the public school in Dorset, where Lawrence had been headmaster; about his friends, my friends, and inevitably, art.

Larry wanted to paint, so I got him some old oil colors, brushes and a corner in which to work. A primitive like Iraklis, he painted lively, childlike scenes from his past: the old brick school he'd once attended, with the children scattered around the yard at recess. Another showed dingy row houses the coal miners lived in, at dawn, dwarfed by the shadow of the towering coal chute and hills of black slag silhouetted like dark monsters against the lightening sky. There was one winter scene, with children sliding down a hill on sleds with wooden runners, the snow taking on the pinks, yellows and greens of the sunset behind them.

When Larry and I finished work for the day, we'd have an *ouzo* on the terrace. Then, he started staying for dinner. And one windy, moonless night in August, he stayed until morning. And the next. The third day he moved in with his clothes, toothbrush and a box of family treasures, including his grandfather's gold pocket watch and his grandmother's silver teapot. In the mornings we'd make love and he'd brew tea in the silver pot and bring me a cup in bed. Days we'd work – I in my studio and he in the old barn we'd converted into a workspace for him. For a time our life together seemed charmed.

After dinners well lubricated with *retzina*, we'd play gin rummy or crazy eights, while Pink Floyd or the Rolling Stones wailed from tapes Larry had duplicated back in Dorset. And each night before we blew out the lamps, Larry read me a chapter from *Winnie the Pooh*. It was a struggle for him to sound out unfamiliar words, and when it bore no fruit, I cued him so he could continue. All his life he had hidden the fact that he couldn't read. The British school system either ignored or was unaware of his dyslexia and let him slide by year after year, until at sixteen, bitter with despair and failure, he finally dropped out. Now he was reading about Pooh and Piglet and Christopher Robin – "Tut, tut, it looks like rain." – and he'd laugh, delighted at both the whimsy generated by these classic tales and by his own growing powers.

I have never been very fond of card playing or rock music, and by the time we'd get to bed I was often exhausted from the day's compromises and would fall like a stone into deep slumber, while he hung there in the middle of a sentence, trying to sound out a word. And he'd wake me, insisting I stay awake despite my bone-aching weariness, until he'd labored through the chapter.

About a month or two into the relationship, it began to dawn on me that I was rapidly losing touch with who I was and what my needs were, and I tried to separate a little and get back to my original rhythms. He sensed the change, and the once soft looks retreated little by little and sinister, side-long glances took their place. Then came emotional abuse and the threat to my life that finally released fear from its lair in the pit of my stomach and sent it on its final, spinning rampage.

An intense loneliness descended. Instead of seeking help, I avoided talking about it with other friends. I was ashamed that this could be happening to me, and I feared that if he were to find out I had "told" on him, he would surely hurt me. I experienced a dark, smouldering anger that I could not release, again out of fear. I thought things would get better if I could avoid doing or saying things that might upset him. Gradually, the world about me took on an air of unreality. There was that normal world out there on the other side of a gray, gauze curtain, where people lived ordinary lives; then there was my world this side of the curtain, gut-wrenchingly intense, engulfed in dread of an evil force that was totally out of my control.

Late one afternoon I came home from the beach to find Larry and an American friend of ours happily inebriated on the terrace. The garden had not been watered and the rabbits gasped in their hot cage with nothing to eat or drink. These two projects had been Larry's idea, and though we shared gardening chores, the rabbits were his responsibility solely.

Who can predict what will tip the scales and allow long pent-up emotions to erupt? For me, it was those rabbits lying with mouths gaping, breathing hard in the heat. The anger I'd been holding in due to fear exploded finally. And so, ultimately, did the violence I knew was coming, and somehow was incapable of escaping. When Larry told Jon to leave, I watched as our friend, oblivious to the circumstances, turned and left me to my fate. "Go into the house," Larry said.

An interesting thing about fear. One begins to think very clearly, very focused. I knew I could not go into that house where I'd be cornered. When I said calmly that no, I was going to sleep in town that night, he moved to push me inside. I jumped beyond his reach and ran down the path toward the gate. Before I could reach it he grabbed me. I had a thought that he might give me a black eye, and almost obediently his fist punched into my face. I was aware that he could break my head open on the dry stone wall, but before that thought became manifest, I had the presence of mind to call out in Greek for help. "*Boítheia!*" My neighbor Michalis heard me and yelled back something I didn't understand. It didn't matter that I didn't understand, only that Larry did. And he understood only one thing: that he had lost face again and in front of witnesses. He released me. I ran off toward town, my dress torn and dirty, long hair matted from salt water and the struggle near the wall. Later, while combing it, great wads clung to the tines, falling out in clumps from fear. In his despair and shame, Larry returned to the house and vented his rage in my studio, kicking in two oil paintings and shattering a stained glass window I had made and treasured. In two days he was gone from the island.

While I have long since dealt with the codependent issues that led me to involve myself with a person who was obviously so bad for me, the point of relating all this here is singular: at my darkest moment of peril, someone called out . . . and most probably saved my life.

*   *   *

Two years later, I met this woman Maria, who was suffering the same experience in essence, only much worse in actuality, because of its repetitiveness and long history. I felt shamed and bewildered that fear – in this case of being afraid again – had paralyzed me at a time when just one shout might have changed the course, if not of her life of abuse (perhaps there was good reason why she hadn't gone to her father for help), then of that one isolated moment, a moment that could have, as well as any of them, been her last. But all my empathy a few hours before had not meant a thing.

"It all happened so quickly!" Iraklis tried to ease my guilt. "If we had interfered it might have made things worse."

"Might have made things worse for us." I countered.

Then, it was as if the scales had dropped, and I was able to see, unmasked, one of the wretched faces of evil, to apprehend the chill and heartless germ of its darkness. Perhaps in the final analysis, it was our own darkness that we all abhorred. "I have no heart," Maria had said. Yes, it was *fear* that was the core of evil, untransformed by love; the shadow unshaped, fathomless, frigid . . . and silent except for the hopeless, naked pounding of the heart.

That night, like the great, deep gulf itself, the olive grove became polluted with the cold breath of fear, so that even the cicadas hid themselves under the gnarled bark of old trees; and silence filled the valley; and every bending blade of grass, every shifting twig could be sensed; until the red moon sank finally into poisoned water and disappeared; and sleep, heavy and acrid with longing, came at last.

Chapter Four

Two Nuns

"Who hears the dragon's roar now?
Perhaps, after all, humankind will inherit
everything that shines. For all night
God enjoys laboring song sung somewhere
with artless abandon."
— Anagram

TWO OR THREE KILOMETERS INLAND FROM THE *HÓRA*, a sprawling cluster of small farms linked by a labyrinth of unpaved roads and paths culminates in the central square of the tiny village of Ano Mera. The large flagstone square surrounded on three sides by restaurants and cafes is flanked on its fourth by the imposing white wall of a monastery where a few monks live away their days. If the cafes form the heart of village life, the monastery serves as its soul, for the simple reason that it houses the village church and provides, through its abbot, the parish priest.

Another monastery — a convent for women — sits a short distance outside the village limits, high on a hill near the ruins of an old fort. As I approached the village, walking from the main town along the winding paved road cutting through the center of the island, I could see the convent in the distance. It sat white against the brown hillside, tilting slightly toward the sea, as if it had been pushed off balance by a shifting of the foundation. Or perhaps it was from spending years leaning into the prevailing north wind that troubles the peace of that side of the island for several months of the year; leaning into the wind, resisting it, unlike the olive trees that bent in acquiescence, or like the monastery in the village, upright and protected by the piety of the villagers. From my vantage point on the winding road, the whitewashed convent resembled a patch of wild daisies leaning toward the sea, the blue dome of its chapel emerging like a morning-glory out of their midst.

A half-hour later I was walking through the entryway, a small opening in the thick iron door, that was locked every night with a rusty key large enough to knock any intruder senseless. Inside the gate, a single eucalyptus tree chattered in the wind and shaded part of the large central courtyard bordered by a double tier of cells. The convent had been built a century ago to house thirty or forty nuns. But only two lived there now: Sister Seraphine, a wizened crone in her sixties, and Sister Kyriaki, about to turn fifty, as round and tightly packed as an onion. Except for the windswept convent they shared, these two were devoid of any common ground upon which to sustain a relationship, except conflict.

Never still for long, Sister Seraphine swept around the convent, her long habit flying in the wind, muttering to herself in her dark, whiskey voice, low and beady as a duck's. Short and wiry, she careened into her tasks like a bent torpedo, or on quieter days, simply leaned into them, as the convent leaned into the wind.

Watching her fly about reminded me of when we kids fed loaves of Wonder Bread to the flock of ducks that swam up and down the shore of the lake where we grew up. The ducks would grab a piece of bread, shake it violently, swallow some and be off to another before finishing the first. Seraphine dashed around the courtyard, bent over her short-handled broom, leaving no corner or crevice in the flagstones untouched. But before she could sweep the pile of dirt into the trash, some thought would take her, robes flying, into the chapel, where she began to fill the box near the doorway with a new supply of beeswax candles; then, leaving it teetering on the edge of the table, she dashed to the oil lamps and refilled them, but without putting in new wicks, because she had suddenly spied some tourists dressed in shorts or too-short skirts, or with bare shoulders, who had just entered, and she unceremoniously swept them outside, raising her voice, telling them that they could not enter the Holy Place naked, and that besides, it was closing time thanks be to God, casting a menacing eye on them as she quacked her orders.

With the startled tourists sufficiently cowed, she rushed back inside
to dust the icons, to wipe off the greasy marks of kisses, to clean first
the glass protecting the Holy Mother, then to kiss it and clean it again.
On she moved to St. John the Baptist, unabashedly holding his own
severed head on a plate, and last she cleaned the glass protecting Christ
Enthroned. Even in her obeisance, the icons seemed to be more pieces
of Wonder Bread, and she barely paused to touch the glass with her
lips before she was off to the next, all the time quacking to herself,
to the icons, to the miscreant tourists, and to the insufferable wind
howling outside, which at that very moment was raising great eddies
of dust from the pile of undisposed debris she had left in the courtyard, swirling it smack up against the closed door of Sister Kyriaki.

Sister Kyriaki was a painter and the one I most often came to see,
although visiting with Kyriaki meant a visit with Seraphine as well,
who always just happened to drop by shortly after my arrival. Kyriaki
was almost as wide as she was tall and, like Seraphine, was covered
entirely, except for her round moon face, in a long black habit and
wimple, on which a small red cross was embroidered just above her
brow. Her confined features seemed to have emerged out of a mighty
block of marble, while Seraphine's had been painstakingly carved from
a piece of gnarled olive wood. They were a strange pair to be rattling
around in this old convent, just the two of them: stone and stick, moon
and Mars, queen bee and drone; milk, not quite warm enough and
wine, aged just a bit too long.

Kyriaki kept her door shut most of the morning in order to discourage
Seraphine from disturbing her painting. Word had spread among the
tourists that the nun out at the village painted pictures you could buy
for a song, and lately her sales had increased so much she had to work
constantly to keep up with the demand. Her paintings were primitive
in a sophisticated sense. That is, she had studied painting before becoming a nun, had earned her DEEploma, as she called it. I asked
her once how she ended up here, all alone except for one other nun
with whom she didn't get along. Why hadn't she been assigned to live
in one of the flourishing convents – like the one on the neighboring
island of Tinos that attracted thousands of visitors each year?

It was impossible for her to be in an active community, she said,
because she did not fit in with the life. Still, she loved God and wanted
to devote her life to his service. But she wanted to paint as well. It
was agreed then, that she would come to this small convent where
she could work freely at her art, provided she limit herself to painting

religious subjects. So she had begun to paint small icons of the saints, figures with underdeveloped limbs and large heads with enormous eyes that stared impassively out at the viewer in identical, blank expressions.

She did it all in a small workspace at the end of the room that served as her kitchen. There she had set up a rickety field easel facing the light from the window of the closed door. At the opposite end of the room, beyond a divider, was the simple kitchen with a two-burner gas plate and small sink. With the exception of the kitchen area itself, paintings were propped all over, paintings of all sizes, some obvious duplicates of others. There were St. John the Evangelist and St. Nicholas with his white hair and beard. And over on another wall St. George on his white steed, reared above the emerald green dragon with white teeth bared and red forked tongue flickering as it writhed upward in its last throes.

Passing into the main room through a low archway, I'd come upon even more paintings, which gave the room a cluttered feeling with its heavy mahogany table and paper doilies. A folding screen closed off one end, whose shadows revealed only the foot of a narrow, uncomfortable-looking bed.

One day I saw a painting I hadn't noticed before, completely different from all the rest. It was larger, for one thing – almost a meter in length – and it showed the Virgin Mary "asleep" on her bier with all the saints, angels and heavenly host gathered around. There were earth-bound figures present too, the only mourners, judging from their pained expressions. And above the bier, the head and torso of the ascended Christ rose out of a radiant cloud with hands extended downward to receive his mother's soul, depicted by the figure of a tiny, naked baby rising aloft. The entire painting pulsated with color, color caught in the pattern formed by the multitude of figures gathered to witness the event of Mary's Assumption.

I was interested in buying the painting and asked her price. Ten drachmas, she shrugged, indicating by giving the price of a loaf of bread, that the painting was priceless, a treasure inspired by God that she would probably never part with. I was disappointed, but she was firm; Kyriaki was sorry, but she would not sell this painting. I didn't pursue it; I knew how it felt when I didn't want to sell a work of my own.

The next time I visited, about a month or two later, the painting was still there, and Kyriaki was still unwilling to sell. Again, I didn't press the issue. But a year later, when I went to see her just before Easter, it was gone. Someone had finally found a price that she couldn't resist.

And it must have been considerable, because behind the folding screen I noticed a thick, new mattress and box spring, and in the kitchen, the two- burner gas plate had been replaced by a full-sized range, complete with oven. In the corner a small refrigerator hummed, and on the counter the remains of a joint of meat sat on a white plate. The meat perhaps was the strongest emblem of Kyriaki's growing worldliness. Eating meat during Holy Week is forbidden by the Orthodox Church.

The painting had been freed from the stifling home of its birth. And Kyriaki, its mother, having been compensated for her loss, went back to her icons and waited obediently, albeit dispassionately, for another rare and transcendent coupling with her Lord.

Before I left, I paid a visit to the convent chapel. Inside, Seraphine was chanting in a high, parched voice, pecking at the leaves of the Psalter on the revolving wooden rack before her like an enormous cormorant. I remembered how she once elbowed her way into a store where I was paying for my purchases and, not waiting her turn, asked Ioannis, the proprietor, if he had any frames for photographs.

When he asked her what she wanted to frame, she seemed embarrassed and then, with some reluctance, pulled out of her black satchel a five-by-seven photograph of a rather severely smiling young woman. It was, of course, Seraphine herself. Seraphine wanted a picture of herself to look at, a picture of her youth, which had vanished long before the day she took her final vows as a bride of Christ.

The villagers snickered at her eccentricities, made jokes and gossiped about her. For it had been said more than once that Seraphine drank. I found that hard to believe, considering her unflagging energy. But I supposed that she could have pulled it off by allowing herself only a drop at measured intervals throughout the day; that might explain why she moved so fast and left so much unfinished. I could just imagine her with so many icons dusted, one thimbleful of Metaxa; four lamps cleaned and filled, another thimbleful; Psalms one hundred twelve through one hundred thirty chanted, a quick gulp in the damp shadows of the pews from a brandy bottle hidden in the folds of her long habit.

But nobody I knew had actually seen her in a state of intoxication, which indicated this story might be nothing more than idle gossip. On the contrary, Seraphine did everything she was supposed to do, followed all the rules, even though it seemed she did so more out of love for the letter of the rule than for its spirit.

One day I was invited to attend a memorial service for the wife of a friend who had died the previous month. Because the village church had been scheduled for something else that day, the service had to be held in the convent chapel. A priest was summoned from the *hóra*, and the nuns would act as cantors. The whole affair was very somber, and the two women entered easily into the spirit of the occasion. Even though they had no personal attachment to the dead woman, their faces, like those of the mortals in Kyriaki's painting, registered in stylized sadness the words of supplication they intoned. Later, outside, a lighter mood prevailed. The men lit up cigarettes and downed cognac passed by the family of the deceased. Then we were all invited upstairs to the Abbess's quarters for coffee.

The Abbess no longer existed, but her rooms remained as a kind of shrine to the last one, whose starched visage gazed severely out from a life-sized oil portrait above the wooden bench in the parlor. There were so many people that I joined an overflow in the bedroom, where I sat on the impossibly hard mattress of the Abbess's bed. Beside it a wooden table covered in a faded cloth displayed a small brass crucifix, a candle, and a bouquet of dried weeds stuck in an empty Gilby's Gin bottle (perhaps in somewhat backhanded homage by Seraphine).

I was glad to be there in that strange room and not in the parlor, where they were all taking care to be on their best behavior, and where I could occasionally glimpse Kyriaki and Seraphine passing sweets and thick coffee with all the formality and bearing of that long-departed Abbess and who, from the uncharacteristic dignity of their expressions, I surmised they were both secretly pretending to be.

Even at the most somber of occasions, such as this memorial, it is hard to squelch the humor of Greeks for long, and in the relaxed atmosphere of the Abbess's bedroom, the wisecracks flew back and forth with muffled laughter as each tried to top the other. One farmer, half serious for a moment, wondered aloud why humankind feared death so much. A woman next to him, her thick, brown hands rocking the top of her cane, said that she definitely thought we should greet death gratefully; because life calls for so much hard work, a good rest is welcome. Another farmer, her husband, and accustomed to using her as a foil, said that, on the contrary, he thought people were so afraid of death because they suspected there was much more work on the other side! Recognizing this truth in the unending toil of their lives, the bedroom exploded in guffaws.

So, there I was in that obscure little convent on an island in the middle of the Aegean Sea on the globe of the world, itself a mere speck in the relentless wheeling of the universe – there, surrounded by Greeks laughing at death, and I was laughing too.

And we were all being served by two nuns putting on airs in empty rooms. I wondered which of them in the end would be greater in the kingdom, at the same time understanding the meaninglessness of such a question. Like the figures in Kyriaki's painting, we all – the farmers and their wives, the bearded priest, the nuns and I – were gathered there that day in supplication for the "assumption" of the dead woman's soul. What a colorful and rich pattern we presented with all our foibles, secret pains, triumphs and failures.

In a moment of shared hilarity, a kind of grace had bound us without our even knowing or understanding it. At that moment death had seemed less a fearsome separation from the world, than an inevitable and celebratory invitation to unite once again with the source – the very ground – of our being.

We had laughed at death. Perhaps our creator laughed at death too, though not out of mirth, as we had . . . but joy.

Chapter Five

Gift

"None learned the art of archery from me who did not
make me, in the end, the target."
— Saadi of Shiraz, 13th Century

"It is ironic that the one thing that all religions recognize
as separating us from our creator — our very self-consciousness — is also
the one thing that divides us from our fellow creatures."
— Annie Dillard

"Well, now that we have seen each other," said the Unicorn," if you'll believe
in me, I'll believe in you. Is that a bargain?"
— Lewis Carroll
Through the Looking Glass

THIS MORNING EARLY, I WALK INTO TOWN AND HEAD
*straight for the vegetable market. There they are, what I expected to find —
carrots, freshly dug young carrots, their long tails of wispy greens spilling
over the edge of the open display case. I ease my way into the crowd
of women filling their bags with produce, and I pick out a large bagful
of the choicest carrots. On the way home I stop to catch my breath at
the top of the steps near the road. Countless trips up the steep hill have
taken me past this spot, yet I have never once paused to notice the field
beyond the wall. This bright morning I take in all the detail. How the
field is bounded on two adjacent sides by the back walls of whitewashed*

houses on the edge of town; how stone walls separate the the other two sides from the steps I am climbing and from the road that encircles the town at their top; how the field at one end is filled with rubble, the crumbling foundation of an old barn and piles of building materials that must have been stored there a long time, judging from the weeds that grow in profusion out of the crannies.

I lay the bag of carrots on the wall. Nearby a horse grazes. His white coat is tarnished with age to a grayish-yellow patina. His ribs bulge out as if he had swallowed a birdcage. One foreleg and flank bear a series of parallel scars — remnants of an encounter with barbed wire perhaps. He stops grazing and looks up, immediately catching sight of the inviting greens billowing out of the brown paper bag. He ambles stiffly over to the wall, and I feed the carrots to him. He takes them in his big brown teeth, leisurely drawing each one into his mouth with thick muscular lips, nibbling them down to the tips of their bright green beards.

"Thank you." I whisper.

*   *   *

My friend Markos had invited me to drop by his house for coffee and a talk. But it was he who always did most of the talking, it turned out, and I who listened – and with much attention too, as if I were listening to the wisdom of the Buddha himself. Markos's merry demeanor and portly frame reminded me of the Buddha, of the Laughing Buddha, in fact, a mahogany figurine given my parents as a wedding gift that sat for years on a corner shelf high above my father's easy chair. Only Markos's height, nearing six feet, and the distinguished appearance of his graying beard and mustache belied any attempt to imagine him as the Buddha, whom I had always seen pictured as being short in stature and completely hairless. Santa Claus, maybe; when it erupted, Markos's laughter displayed the kind of detached merriment that the jolly old elf, had he embodied the soul of the Buddha, might have shown the world.

My own inner world seemed to be sinking into a deep abyss. I was just turning thirty, and it was painfully apparent that I still had not discovered a place for myself. A part of me longed for the secure niche of marriage – husband, house, the two children. But in another corner a small flame was igniting that, as far as I could see, would deprive me of such comforts. That flame wanted to travel, to have adventures, to meet interesting people and, through art, somehow give shape and voice to the mysterious longings deep within me.

But how could I choose between these two needs? And when did it seem necessary to actually choose between a family and a life devoted to art? It was a question typical of the period in which I was nurtured: the fifties and early sixties. A stranger on a Boston street once summed up my dilemma. As I hurried to an art class he stopped me and asked to see the painting I was carrying. After studying it a few seconds, he turned and said with a wistful smile:

"It's good. You will be an artist someday if you can keep from getting married."

It wasn't only my personal world that was unsettled. I also had become aware of the increasing dis-ease and chaos of the times I lived in. Wars, large and small, flared up and sputtered over the globe like defective fireworks. The compounding crime rate in cities echoed growing social unrest. Most ominous of all was my growing awareness of how our carefully crafted solution to one problem invariably opened up new and more complex problems to be solved: medical advances lengthened lives, but could not guarantee the quality of those lives. New drugs sometimes left side effects that were more dreadful than the disease they were designed to treat. I watched how advances in science and technology provided by the splitting of the atom caused us all to contemplate for the first time the possibility of our own collective dissolution. In the deepest sense of tragedy, our finest, most noble efforts seemed ultimately destined to fail, to actually turn against us, in fact, like some Jekyll turned Hyde.

Worse still, it seemed that no one, and I least of all, was capable of reaching out to another in an act untainted by self-interest. I became acutely aware of my own self-enhancement and ego-preservation in everything I did – from writing a letter home, to having friends for dinner, to painting a landscape. What was this ego anyway? And who was I – anyway?

It was a time of such insecurity and bleakness that I could not see or hear or feel any of the goodness in the world or in myself. The daily news only compounded my depression, so I stopped listening to the radio and reading newspapers. I buried myself instead in books on psychology, seeking the thread to lead me out of the labyrinth. I sat long hours that first winter in the *hóra* crocheting bags and hats and pillow covers, my mind ranging far into the past, my fingers moving swiftly and automatically through the intricate patterns. I was thankful for my friends, especially Markos, as the exposure to all he had to teach began to nudge me out of the darkness.

Though I tell the story of my awakening here, I never did fully hear his. All I knew about Markos was that he had once been an advisor in the Greek government. Divorced with three grown children, he shared an apartment with his aging father in the center of Athens. From June through November he lived on Mykonos.

Our visits fell into a once-a-week pattern. After I had done the shopping and checked for mail at the post office, I rang the bell of his cluttered flat near the windmills. Always his greeting was the same:

"Ah, *yiá soú*, Nansoula! (Markos was one of the few Greeks who didn't call me Anna, adding instead the feminine diminutive "-oula" to my given name). "*Tí káneis* – how are you? Come in, come in." With eyes crinkled in a smile, hand extended, Markos – and his big Doberman crowing and dancing on hind legs in the background – created an altogether chaotic but unequivocal welcome.

Then came the offer of a coffee and the lighthearted chit-chat about the weather or the tourists or the rising price of bread while we waited for water to boil and we could adjourn to his book-filled living room. This room was cozy and well buffered from the northwest wind that whipped in from the sea during November storms. Often the aroma wafted through the room of chickpea or lentil soup simmering on the space heater between two heavily-draped north windows.

With steaming cups of Nescafe and milk we settled into huge overstuffed sofas, draped with some of the island's woven blankets. Markos sat back with a playful glance. "Well, so that's the way it is, is it?"

In my self-consciousness, this common figure of speech took on serious undertones, and I wondered what on earth he was talking about when he asked me that. Was he merely shifting the gears of the conversation into more serious areas? Or was I so transparent that he could read my mind? And I thought, no, Markos, that isn't the way it is, and began awkwardly to relate all that had been going on in my life the previous week – all my doubts, fears, dashed expectations.

When I was done, he talked, gradually chipping away at the rampart of certainty that kept my world, however hopeless, in place. This "certainty" told me that what my five senses experienced of the world was the only truth – that what I saw (or heard, or tasted, or touched, or smelled) was all there was. The idea that there might be other realities perceived with as yet undiscovered senses had never occurred to me. So all was not as I perceived it, no. I need not be the victim of the circumstances around me.

"Have you always been so serious, Nansoula?" And then he leaned back and laughed, as the Laughing Buddha sitting above my father's chair had laughed in perpetual mirth at what unfolded in our living room. So Markos laughed at my suffering, laughed me out of it, in fact, with his merriment, with his peculiar brand of detached warmth, with his promise of other realities. He was a sage sitting at the mouth of his cave, and I was a seeker intent on absorbing truth and, thus, hope at his feet.

For two years I borrowed his books from shelves that lined two sides of the room. Later, in the dim lamplight of my own house, I poured over the ancient words of Lao Tzu, the *Bhagavad Gītā*, the exalted poetry of the *Upanishads*, the Christian mystics, St. Theresa of Avila and St. John of the Cross and the comforting congruence of East and West in the writings of Thomas Merton.

But the first book Markos lent me, and the one with the most transforming effect, was a collection of ancient teaching stories *The Way of the Sufi*, written by revered sages of the Sufi sect of Islam. The names of their illustrious authors – Jalaludin Rumi, Attar of Nishapur, Eli- Gazali and Omar Khayyam – seemed bathed in the scents of jasmine and sandalwood and rolled off the tongue with a gratifying sensuousness. Surviving the ravages of translation through the ages, these were tales told in the language of poetry and myth with disarming subtlety and humor.

Reading the Sufi stories was my first exposure to anything spiritual since I was in college. My head filled with questions and doubts engendered by a sophomore philosophy class, I had rejected any form of religion or spirituality. The fragile house of cards of childhood beliefs came tumbling down.

Ten years later, after living in a world I had stripped of any spiritual dimension, I couldn't have been more ripe for the clear imagery and gentle humor of the Sufis. All those years I had been my own "prime mover," the altogether inept captain of my ship. After ten years of foundering in the sea of that delusion, I was about to sink. In the little volume of Sufi stories, Markos had thrown out the lifeline that drew me back into the channel leading to quieter waters that I had been seeking all along.

"Are you a Sufi?" I asked him when I returned his book. I couldn't help but notice his resemblance to the Sufi sages who in the book were described as being wise and inscrutable people, trailed by their ever-present dervishes. I was so excited and awe-struck by this possibility that I could barely sputter out the question.

Markos laughed, shook his head, no, he was not a Sufi. But he said that he felt he was on a path that was leading him toward enlightenment.

Enlightenment: there was that word – to shed light on truth, my dictionary said, to free from ignorance. Enlightenment: the word some of my acquaintances spoke about with a capital "E" as they tore off little corners of blotting paper impregnated with LSD. Enlightenment: a word filled with hope; a word that was also ripe with the romance of being out of the ordinary, an escape I longed for in my despair for this moribund world and the fearful ordinariness of my inner life.

I was calmed by these visits with Markos, and by the *idea* of enlightenment even though its reality eluded me. I was consoled by the hope that Truth, whatever it was, lay somehow just beyond the invisible curtain separating this world as I perceived it from other realities that were equally and maybe even more valid.

I was also calmed by the promise that serenity would come with detachment. Or was it the other way around? Anyway, all the books I was reading talked about detachment. But detachment from what? For a time the prospect of being detached from the lives of others around me seemed attractive; to be better than they, to sit with Markos at the mouth of his cave, to know something others did not know; to gaze with him in perfect serenity while the whirlwind world played out its destiny around us; to watch with Markos's same benevolent mirth the incessant turning of the universe.

Oh, yes, I could do that – and can still when I forget certain essential things. But life has ways of pulling me away from its periphery and back into its vortex where I must once again deal with the world on its own terms, with what it still has to teach me, not what, in my self exaltation, I have to teach it. Much to my disappointment, I had to admit that my understanding was still firmly buried in the deepest bowels of the earth, too coarse to gambol with the angels high in the ether.

It was the detachment issue that seemed to mark a turning point for both Markos and me. So subtly at first that I didn't notice it, we both were changing.

As the months followed one after the other, Markos began to share with me more of his thoughts about people he knew, some of whom I was acquainted with as well. Where at one time he had gently chided me for criticizing a person, he now freely indulged in the same. He recreated, word for word, how he played with people, outsmarted them – the taxi driver, the teller at the bank, the tobacconist where he bought his cigarettes.

He charmed everyone; he was aware of it and seemed to relish these encounters and in telling me about them. He "knew" something others did not know, was privy to being "in the world, but not of it," as the literature of enlightenment professes its elect to be. He played with people's vulnerabilities, their sure confidence in the domain of the five senses, tickling them with gentle and not-so-gentle challenges just as he had done with me. And when in their confusion they couldn't answer him, he confounded them even more by speaking nonsense, playing with words, with certainty, with them.

For a long time I laughed with him, basking in my position as confidante of one of the elect. I even fancied that I understood what he was saying and that I "knew" Truth as well. I treasured my usurped position atop Mount Olympus without once trying to understand how I had arrived and why I really didn't belong there.

On some level I must have understood how pride separated me from people, for that particular form of detachment was surely engendered by pride. What I began to realize was how my self-imposed detachment seemed to wrap around me even more tightly the shroud of cotton batting that shielded me from my pain. Hope that my pain would cease was about to cause me, a feeling person, to cease; I saw my capacity for empathy and compassion slipping away. As consciousness of my own faltering became more vivid, I began to sense that Markos was tipping dangerously toward the precipice as well.

He had been writing about seeking enlightenment through meditation. There are countless manuals written on that subject, but Markos's book had one distinguishing purpose: to demonstrate that meditation could be learned without a teacher. Markos had become convinced from his own experience that a teacher, a living, breathing flesh-and-blood guide was not necessary.

By the time he told me about his project I had read enough on the subject to know that if one thing was emphasized by all, it was the peril of trying to learn the discipline of meditation without a guide. Not only could the practice provide baffling and sometimes frightening images, but left to its own devices, the mind could fool itself into believing much that was untrue, and because of the nature of self-deception, many danger areas would pass unrecognized. If I felt wiser than Markos at this point, it was wisdom gleaned from books, not experience. Mine was the wisdom of the naive, the uninitiated, but wisdom nevertheless of a healthy fear.

One day while he was in the middle of one of his stories about outmanuvering someone whom I happened to know, I dared a rather oblique confrontation. In Markos's not-so-carefully concealed disdain, I began to clearly see my own growing hardness of heart. The impulse to laugh with him was strong. Yet I couldn't help seeing our folly. I could no longer laugh with him; nor could I just listen and say nothing. It wasn't that I had begun to dislike Markos. Indeed, I cared enough to fear for him, but I hesitated to come right out and criticize him. After all, to judge Markos, to presume to know more than he, seemed a sure way of setting myself up for a fall. Nevertheless, I interrupted his story and said lamely, "You must be very proud, Markos."

Other than a fleeting look of surprise, he gave no indication that he had understood my warning.

Summer came and another winter. Markos spent more and more time at his flat in Athens, making only short visits to the island. Though I still occasionally stopped by, I now left feeling confused and even a little forlorn. I missed the old Markos whose wisdom I had been so sure of – or maybe I missed the old me, and the innocence that is satisfied with easy answers you can read about in books.

In time I heard that he had undergone minor surgery in Athens. And next came the news that he had suffered a nervous breakdown following the surgery. When I visited him in Athens during his recovery I saw a totally different Markos – a broken man, a man enveloped in such a deep sorrow that all he could do was sigh. He told me he had sought out everyone he thought he had ever offended and had apologized. Whether these people had been aware of any injury or not didn't seem to matter to him. His sadness at his own folly was deep and genuine. It was the humility of a man who had seen himself completely stripped of masks. I felt an incredible tenderness for my friend who had fallen so far and so hard, as well as a renewal of trust in – and healthy respect for – unknown, unseen forces.

Was it Nemesis, the goddess of divine retribution? Was there really a divine force, and had it humbled Markos forcibly? Was it a karmic debt suddenly come due? Had he ever been as wise as I had imagined him to be? Or was he just now beginning to attain wisdom? If pride separates us from one another – from God – does humility unify us, heal us? These were the questions I asked myself in the wake of my friend's personal "trial by fire." And the answer emerged that perhaps what opened the door to enlightenment was to experience to the marrow of our bones our incompleteness as individuals, to fathom at last our connection to everyone, to everything.

Markos rarely visited the island after that. He was changing, and so was I. It was time for me to give up the unearned mountain peaks and begin trekking the rolling foothills of living that had suddenly become vibrant with possibility.

Even the past took on new meaning, for though I had proven myself too coarse to gambol with the angels, perhaps they had not been made of too fine a substance to descend from the ether and play with me.

*   *   *

One night, about a year before his breakdown, Markos invited me to his house for dinner. For the occasion he had prepared one of his specialties, a delicious dish with eggs and sausages, spiced with curry and covered in melted cheese. We sat in the living room after dinner drinking coffee and smoking acrid Greek cigarettes. I don't remember what we – or later he – talked about. We might have talked about the Sufis, or Christ, or an amusing encounter he'd had with someone that day. I don't remember, and it doesn't matter. But when I left around nine I felt relaxed, mellowed by the peculiar peace I always seemed to catch from him then like some divinely communicable healing. I was glad I'd thought to wear the old fisherman's sweater that was just right for warding off the chill wafting in from the sea on that still April night. My mind became intent on some idea we'd been discussing as I climbed the hill heading home.

Rather than taking the paved road with its numerous switchbacks, I usually followed a path that led straight up the hill surrounding the *hóra*. As I climbed the first steep steps approaching the edge of town, I heard a strange sound. It came from the other side of the dry-stone wall to my left, apparently from the field beyond it – a shuffling, rock-crunching sound coming closer and closer. The wall was almost six feet high, its top looming well above my head, so that I couldn't see what was making the sound. A little farther up the steps I found a foothold where I could step up and look over.

In the field, heading fast in my direction, I saw a small flock of sheep. How strange it was that they weren't afraid of me, I thought; sheep usually flee from humans, as if in their unease, they somehow consciously know (unlike humans) the purpose of their lives. But when these sheep reached the wall they wheeled around. Then I understood: far from coming to *see me*, the sheep were being driven by something until they had come upon the wall and my wide dark eyes peering over at them – driven to the wall until they had to turn, stumbling and bleating in confusion, to head back in the opposite direction, creating a wide swath around the lone figure of a horse who was walking quickly toward me.

When it reached the wall the horse put its head over and leaned down to me. I held my hand up to his nose and touched the soft, warm velvet around his nostrils. The moon, brightening the sky with its near fullness, cast a blue tinge to his white coat, and his eyes were large and liquid dark as they looked down at me. I reached up impulsively and touched the area just under his forelock. Beneath the coarse hair my fingers found a little cowlick spiraling up about a half an inch. I wanted very much to get closer so that I could stroke his head more easily. It was impossible with the high wall, so I continued up the stairs to where they met the road encircling the town. This wall was no higher than my waist. The horse followed me. Again I stroked his head and the soft velvet of his nose; I talked to him and told him how beautiful he was in the moonlight, how happy I was to be there, to stroke his long neck and to feel such closeness with him.

Then he did such an odd thing: he reached down suddenly and took the hem of my sweater in his teeth and started to tug at it. I pulled the sweater out of his grasp, afraid it would tear, but he bent for it again and again. The sweater's hem, stretched taut from his teeth to my waist, remained the boundary I could not manage to pass – in acquiescence to what seemed to be an unmistakable invitation to cross over the wall and enter the field!

Just then a car came by, its headlights sweeping a cascade of light over us as it passed. This sudden and unexpected intrusion of artificial light caused me to become aware also of the large globe of a street lamp directly above us. How like a spotlight it seemed; how odd the Greeks in the taxi must have thought it to see Anna (and they would have recognized me) standing there talking to a horse (there surely would have been jokes too, the women tittering behind their hands). As always, my imagination soared on the wings of self-consciousness – an old feeling. I gave the horse a last pat on the neck and turned, heading across the road and up more steps that led to the road out to my house. Silly Anna! Silly Horsie! Silly moonlight, bewitching us that way!

Back at the house, I sat at the kitchen table and waited for a pot of mint tea to brew. I felt let down. At first I couldn't define why. But as I allowed the feeling to sink into me I soon recognized an old disappointment. It always followed when I was to experience some wonderful thing, but then out of fear refused to take the risk necessary to claim it.

I remembered an unusual encounter with another white horse on my first, brief trip to the island in 1967. I loved walks, walks where I could freely explore the countryside, meandering at will off the path to walk through the rooms of abandoned houses, pick wild mint from a stream-fed valley, climb with a flock of goats up the remote, rocky paths leading to the summit of the small mountain that dominated the northeast region of the island. I'd take my camera along and a string bag to collect anything that caught my interest – mostly junk, like the weathered wood and rusty pieces of metal to use later in collages. Sometimes a castoff piece of pottery caught my eye, or a bone, beautifully sculpted and bleached by the weather, gleaming against the dark, moist soil of winter. I liked to sit a long time in the shade of old abandoned houses, imagining the generations of farmers who had lived there with their families, the babies born on the platform there where the bed must have been, the meals served from that kitchen fireplace.

That day in 1967, on a long walk out to the lighthouse I had decided to leave the road and climb up some rocks to a plateau that overlooked a small bay. It was a difficult climb over loose stones and past sharp drops. At the top, about fifty feet above the road, I came out around a big boulder almost as tall as I was. Facing south, I could see the white town back in the direction I'd come from, shimmering far in the distance against the ochre hillside surrounding it. I was miles from there, off a winding dirt road that led to the lighthouse on the bleak, northern tip of the island. Even though all the land was owned by someone and used for pasture, no one lived this far out. If I had fallen and injured myself on my way up to the plateau, I wouldn't have been found for days.

Because of this remoteness I wasn't expecting to see the horse. His white neck, back and rump stood out starkly against the deep blue of the sea below and mirrored the scene of the town against the hills in the distance. The horse raised his head from grazing and looked at me with an alert, but peaceful posture, ears standing up and slightly forward – not laid back in alarm. I had no impulse to go near him or to talk to him; we just watched each other for one or two minutes, each of us surprised and curious about the other. Feeling like an intruder in that quiet place, I took my Pentax from where it was slung across my back and snapped a picture of the scene. Then I continued down the other side of the plateau, northward toward the lighthouse.

For a long while after this walk, I remembered how pleasant that brief encounter had been, how peaceful it was so high above the sea, the pristine location, that plateau, dotted with isolated boulders placed at odd angles by some caprice of nature. The barren ground produced little vegetation in June – only the prickley *angáthi* and graceful Queen Anne's Lace, its blossoms exploding like fireworks, each tiny cluster an image of the main flower. The ground was swept clean and smooth by wind, and with boulders like small monoliths, the plateau had resembled a Japanese garden, a place for meditation like the ones I would read about in Markos's books years later. I often wished that I'd sat down against one of those boulders instead of hurrying on, that I'd spent some time there with pad and ink and colors – all persistent survivors of earlier, more slowly-paced times than the age of the camera.

As I sat thinking at the kitchen table after returning from dinner with Markos, I realized that now I had encountered another white horse and perhaps another opportunity for change. But how differently this creature had acted than the earlier one! How strange that he had come toward me across the field, almost as if he were being driven, just as surely as he had been driving the sheep. What had he wanted me to do when he pulled on my sweater?

The seed of this encounter's importance to me had been planted three years before, when I'd read a book given to me by friends for my birthday. The story, *The Last Unicorn*, was an allegory about the last unicorn on earth, how it had not been a good age for unicorns, how they all must have died off. One section in particular came to mind as I sat at the kitchen table drinking the soothing tea – the section about the hunters who couldn't find any unicorns, and how the great-grandmother of one hunter had actually seen a unicorn once in her youth, how she always cried when she told of it and how she had loved its smell as she sat stroking its sleeping head. As the legends went, unicorns were by nature ferocious fighters and extremely shy of humans. But the woman had received the trust of this unicorn, a gift bestowed only on innocence.

Then I began to cry – for all the chances to allow some special good into my life that I had rejected because of fear of the unknown, or that I might look foolish to others. My inner world up to that point had not been amenable to miracles, filled as it was with such fears. Yet, thanks to my visits with Markos, I had come to accept the possibility that good might dwell in this world, that love and purity existed – if not always in humankind, then in a force or energy we couldn't perceive, an energy that allowed, because it was invisible, the possibility of the miraculous. But that night, as I had done so many times before, I forfeited my chance to experience the miraculous, and fear as always had been the culprit. My attention, deflected to the Greeks in the taxi, to the street lamp, had allowed outer intrusions into my inner experience. Fear: a familiar betrayal, almost too strong an adversary to conquer. Sad, how sad it was how fear kept me, how it kept the world, in chains. I rose, weary and drained, and went to bed.

The following day passed uneventfully. I emerged from this intense introspection like a moth too soon out of its cocoon, my mood still tainted by sticky strands of regret that held me to the failure of the night before and refused to let me forget it and spread my wings into the day. The sun was almost too hot, but good for "ironing" the laundry that flapped on the line. By mid-afternoon I had nearly *returned to my senses:* it occured to me that for a person capable of rational thought, the very idea that the horse had been anything other than someone's plow horse was really a giant step out of reality. And there were places prepared for people who too often confused what was real with what was not.

By five the laundry was down and folded; I'd filled the amphora with water, whitewashed the kitchen floor and taken a bath in a tub of sun-warmed water under the blue sky in the walled-in barnyard. The day had been so filled with tasks I never once ventured into the studio. My rational mind had taken over the dreaming mind, and there could be no paintings that day without dreaming. By six I was on my way to town to do some errands and meet a friend for dinner. After a wonderful meal of fresh fish in a restaurant by the sea, we sat drinking coffee and making plans to meet at the beach in two days. About ten I headed up the hill again.

A full, still moon hung like a plate and lit my way, so bright it cast a shadow. I followed my usual route, the same steps I had climbed the previous night. These nocturnal walks up the hill and out the dirt road to my house were times when my thoughts often went into a kind of focused limbo where no distractions intruded. I loved these walks in the darkness, especially when I got farther out in the country and the stars, free of competition from village lights, stood as bright sentinels right down to the horizon. For all my fears, I never feared the darkness on these walks and never bothered to carry a flashlight. That night as I approached the edge of town, I didn't think about stars, but the landscape I'd begin painting the next morning after breakfast. My mind's eye roamed over the canvas, the colors and textures becoming so clearly delineated that I could almost see the finished painting.

Then he was there, not a foot away from the wall, near the same steps I had climbed the night before. In the aura of the fine meal and relaxed companionship, I hadn't thought of the horse the entire evening. I couldn't believe he was there, yet somehow I wasn't surprised. I greeted him. His head hung over the wall as before, reaching for my hand to nuzzle him.

I continued up the steps to the road where the wall was lower. He followed me, and I stroked his head, searching under his forelock for the spiral cowlick. Then he reached for the hem of my sweater with his teeth, and he pulled.

Yes, the moon was bright and the circle of lamplight even brighter, but this time I didn't care. I sat on the wall and swung my legs over. He turned and slowly walked away, leading me out of the lamplight into a far, darkened corner of the field. I followed him until he stopped and knelt down, lowering himself – awkwardly, as all large four-legged creatures do – to the ground. I sat down and put my arms around his neck, my face very close, touching his. Then his eyes closed, and his great, heavy head slowly lowered into my lap, and he slept.

I don't know how long we sat there, my arms wrapped around the neck of the horse, the weight of his head resting in my lap. I pressed my nose into the crevice behind his right ear. How good he smelled, that sweet, clean horse smell I remembered from childhood when I rode weekends at a nearby stable. I could feel my cheeks were wet, but I wasn't crying; water simply came from my eyes, unchecked. I don't know how long we sat there; I don't know what the town looked like in the moonlight. It was April, and I know there must have been wildflowers. We sat a long time or a short time; all I know is that it happened, and I don't know if it happened; yet I know. I know it did.

The spell was broken ultimately, as it had to be. It was probably the discomfort I slowly became aware of, sitting on the damp ground. When I carefully shifted my position the horse raised his head, momentarily startled out of sleep. I sat very still, and once again he dozed off. But it was no good; the damp ground and my discomfort began to claim my attention; I had to shift again. This time he was fully awake and abruptly rose up on all four legs. It was over. Whatever it was that had held us both in its benevolent embrace had released us to go our separate ways.

I turned and walked back to the wall. When I had crossed it, I looked back. "*Káli níkta*, my friend," I said silently. He was watching me, his dark, liquid eyes and gleaming white body standing out against the dark field in the blue wash of moonlight.

Chapter Six

Barba Manolis

"How shall the heart be reconciled
to its feast of losses?"
— Stanley Kunitz
"The Layers"

WHAT PROPELS A MAN IN THAT FINAL HOUR BACK TO HIS
childhood, to the one place out of all those experienced in a long life,
where he had known nothing but the unquestioned integrity of his
own imagination? What voice calls him back to that time, that place
of innocence? What sense tells him, so that he knows without doubt
that his "being in the world" is about to fragment into its most in-
finitesimal parts; that the place where he had once stood, under the
sun of his own certainty, would soon resound with only the rever-
berating atoms of his final breath — and then, nothing? What is that
something inside us, which is not us, that tells us this: to go home?

From the Journal - August 24, 1977

Barba Manolis was buried yesterday. A week ago he had attended the
panagiri honoring the Assumption of the Virgin, a lavish feastday, second
only to Easter. For the first time in years, to the delight and awe of everyone,
he had danced the Zembékiko — with feeling and surprising agility, con-
sidering his eighty-seven years.
* The next morning back in his house in town, he had wakened feeling*

ill and, without hesitating even for a coffee, he mounted his donkey and set off up the long, winding road out to the family farm. He just managed to get through the gate when he collapsed on the terrace. Somehow, his daughter-in-law Flora got him into bed. But he worsened as the days passed, and he refused all food, despite sometimes heroic efforts to get him to take some nourishment. Of his six daughters, the five who lived on the island ministered to him in shifts. The sixth, Anna, was to arrive later from Athens. I learn that he is ill, and late one afternoon I set out on foot to see him.

*   *   *

"You're going to like your new landlord," Hugh said, as we climbed aboard the bus, a dilapidated Mercedes of unknown vintage. Hugh was an American dropout living on a few drachmas earned from odd jobs. When he wasn't working, I'd find him in one of the waterfront cafes drinking coffee and smoking cigarette stubs he'd saved, perusing with a dignified air an ancient issue of *Barron's*. As a friend and tutor in the simple life who spoke passable Greek, he came along to do the translating.

It was the spring following that first long winter on the island. We were on our way to a farm midway between the *hóra* and the village of Ano Mera. Our mission was to find an old farmer, Manolis Asimomitis, whom everyone called "Barba" Manolis, or "Uncle" Manolis, the familiar term of respect for all men past fifty. We wanted to talk to him about my renting an old farmhouse that belonged to one of his daughters who was temporarily living in the United States.

I paid the four drachma fare while Hugh asked the driver in Greek to let us off at the Asimomitis farm. We settled into a seat near the front. It was four-thirty, nearing the end of siesta, and the bus was almost empty, a fact for which I was grateful as the screaming engine labored in protest up the steep, winding road leading out of town. Ten minutes later, with breaks squealing and clouds of dust billowing around us, we came to a sudden, shuddering halt.

"You, Barba Manolis, here!" the driver offered in English, flashing two gold bicuspids and pointing first at us, then to the left and finally to the door as he swung it open.

The house, which sat low to the left, about a hundred yards from the road, looked deserted. We were perplexed. Everyone had said he would be out at his farm that day – but where? We set off about two hundred yards farther down the valley to ask a neighbor, an old woman sitting on her terrace stringing beans.

"He's there, in his field, plowing," she smiled, pointing to the north-west. Sure enough, we saw in the distance, over several fields and walls, lilliputian figures crisscrossing a triangular field. We thanked the woman and set off down a donkey trail she had pointed out as the quickest way. About ten minutes later, three faces, one middle-aged and wimpled, another old and weathered, and the last, bovine with a white star on its forehead, turned in curiosity to greet the two foreigners.

Hugh introduced me to Barba Manolis and his daughter Marsó, and explained our quest. Not knowing the language, there wasn't much I could say, so I just stood, enthralled with my surroundings and with the old man who, up to a moment ago, had been guiding a ridiculously primitive plow through rocky soil behind a docile Holstein that was ready, I noticed, to be milked.

I guessed that he was in his early eighties. He had a thick, bushy moustache and wore his hat perched backward on his head to keep the hot sun off his bare neck. He had secured his plaid flannel shirt inside his trousers with a striped apron, rolled up and wound around his waist like a cummerbund. His thick, bare feet were sunk up to the ankles in the newly turned soil. But probably his most remarkable feature was the expression in his eyes. They smiled at me out of the deep tracery of wrinkles with such friendliness that they seemed to perceive in a glance every thought I had ever had in my life, and it didn't matter, no, not a twit.

"Welcome," he said, "You mean Vangelo's house up the road? Fine, fine. How long would she like to stay?"

"Tell him for the summer," I said, "but maybe longer."

Our negotiations completed, Barba Manolis and I shook hands on our agreement of seven hundred drachmas rent a month, roughly twenty dollars.

*   *   *

I arrive at the farm. The curtain in the door to the kitchen wafts out over the whitewashed terrace. The small, stooped figure seated on a chair welcomes me. He is in his long woolen underwear, and someone has draped a flannel shirt over his shoulders. After so many hot days unbroken by wind, he says he is enjoying the opportunity to sit outside. From the parlor door I can hear the familiar canned laughter of an ancient "I Love Lucy" re-run, and I have to shout above it for him to hear me. His grand-daughter, Maria, about thirteen years old, emerges from the snare of the

*sitcom to see who belongs to the strange voice shouting at her grand-
father. When she sees me, she shouts as well:* Yiá soū, Anna! *How was
I and I had come to see Barba Manolis, eh? Then Flora, her mother, returns
from milking, hears the commotion and joins in.*

*"Welcome, Anna!" she calls shrilly. "How are you? You came to see Barba
Manolis? He's doing all right, but he won't eat, will you, Babá? Tonight
you will have some chicken and macaroni, eh? Anna, tell him he must
eat, or he won't get well."*

*I imagine that the noise from the television and the raised voices all
speaking at once must be as harrowing to Barba Manolis as it is to me.
But he looks off over the fields, withdrawn into his own thoughts. I ask
Maria to turn down the television. She nods and disappears. Flora chatters
off into the kitchen, and we are left alone.*

*We sit a long time without speaking, just listening to sounds of the
country, frogs chirruping in remnants of a pond below the house, cows
lowing to each other across fields. He smiles and points out a few things,
but that's all. It seems right, the two of us here on the terrace, quiet,
watching the light change.*

*   *   *

Early evening as the sun set was the time to stop work and relax with
an *ouzo* on the terrace. From here I could see four large islands rising
from the sea, under a sky that stretched unbroken to the horizon in
three directions. And it was from this terrace on a rare sleepless night
that I would note the diaphanous cloud of the Milky Way arcing directly
over my house, or so it seemed in that mysterious place of the heart
where everything was benevolent, everything protected, connected and
harmonious.

Some evenings at sunset I would sit with my feet up on the parapet
and be gently roused from my thoughts by a creak of the gate down
by the road. I never even had to look to know who it was. I greeted
him and went to the kitchen for bread and another glass and poured
him an *ouzo*, adding water that exploded the drink into a milky liquid.

I spoke only a few words of Greek then, so these visits were forced
into becoming language lessons. He would start out by pointing at
something nearby:

"Piáta," for example, and I'd repeat "Pee-AH-ta." Then he'd ask for
the word in English, and I'd say "plate," to which he responded
"PLAI-eet," adding with a nod, *"kondá"* – close.

The next one: "*piroūni.*"

"Peer-OO-ni," I'd parrot.

"*Stá 'Anglikā?*"

"Fork."

"For-k" he repeated, softly rolling the "r." " '*Óhi kondá*," he added.

"Not close at all," I agreed.

Then we'd clink glasses and sip the strong anise flavored aperitif until it was time for him to untether his donkey and continue into town. Always before leaving, he'd lay bunches of grapes or tomatoes on the old yellow table, or perhaps some new potatoes he'd just dug up. One evening he left a cucumber that was close to a foot long and almost four inches thick.

"Life is a cucumber," he informed me, his eyes crinkling in a smile and his thick eyebrows bobbing up and down, something he did unconsciously, I noticed, whenever he was pleased with his own joke.

It was Barba Manolis who gave me the name Anna. He had trouble remembering my real name and, since he could neither read nor write, he couldn't picture it in his mind either. "NEHN-si," he'd say, the last syllable barely pronounced. But the foreign sound wouldn't stay in his memory for long and, after several frustrated attempts to remember, he said one day, with an air of finality, that my name would be Anna. Anna, a common, easily remembered Greek name. One of his daughters was named Anna, and Anna was the name of the mother of the Blessed Virgin. A good name, Anna.

Another evening, on the subject of names, I had expressed surprise that he hadn't named his donkey, other than calling it "the donkey." I took the matter in hand and came up with another good Greek name, Maria, forgetting about the Blessed Virgin and not learning until some time later, when my Greek had improved and we were able to converse more easily, that his dead wife's name had been Maria.

"Maria?" he frowned.

"Maria," I said. "It's a wonderful name for a donkey!"

He shrugged with a smile barely visible beneath his thick moustache and crossed himself.

* * *

Flora returns to ask if I would like a plate of chicken, winking toward the old man and making me an unwilling co-conspirator in the unending battle to get him to eat. I know he won't eat, and I tell her politely, no thanks, but I must leave, that I must meet someone in one hour. Barba Manolis says something to her that I don't catch, and she disappears into the kitchen. I linger a few minutes more and then, unable to say good-bye, I tell him that I'll be back in a day or two. I step off the terrace just as Flora rushes out of the kitchen with a burlap sack she presses into my arms. Inside I see about four kilos of potatoes, some zucchini and tomatoes, three round, white cheeses, two small watermelons and a corked wine bottle full of goat's milk: Barba Manolis's final gift to me from his farm.

*   *   *

He had asked me several times to come to his house in town for dinner, but there always seemed to be other conflicting concerns. One night, however, I made it a point to go, afraid that after so many refusals, there would be no more invitations.

He welcomed me at the door and ushered me in. His house was tiny by American standards, but not so unusual on this island, where everything, from the harbor to the single molehill of a mountain, was pared down to human scale. There was a narrow bed to the right as I entered, and to my left, an armoire and large wooden steamer trunk. On the wall above it, the flame of a small oil lamp cast a warm glow on two icons, one of St. George and the other of the Virgin. In the back we stepped down once into the kitchen, located under a sleeping loft and lit by a single bare light bulb. Another narrow bed was tucked beneath the stairs leading up the loft. I guessed he could shelter three or four friendly people, if the need ever arose.

"*Kátse,*" he said, indicating one of the chairs next to the cluttered kitchen table. I asked him if I could help. Pointing to the dish rack near the sink, he said I would find everything I needed to set the table. I took out a couple of forks and plates, two glasses, but with momentary disgust, I discovered that everything was coated with a thin film of grease. Noting that there was only a cold water faucet I guessed the culprit. I tried to overlook it, but the grease film was too much for even my less than fastidious nature. I tried to reason how to handle it. I could quickly rinse off everything, but more cold water wasn't going to help, and if I proceeded to get a towel and wipe off the water-beaded film I might offend, or worse, embarrass my friend. The only alternative, I realized, was to ignore it and proceed as if everything had just come out of a steaming dishwasher. The choice was clear: in a little act of faith, that never disappointed me, I decided that no bad thing could ever pass from Barba Manolis to me, regardless of the circumstances.

In the meantime, it was easy to see where the oily film had come from. He stood at the small gas stove frying some of the sausage his family had made at the November pig killing, and I watched, fascinated at the half-inch or so of hot olive oil and pork fat that bubbled up suddenly around the edges of the eggs he had just poured in. The omelet was soon firm and he slipped it onto a plate, pouring the sizzling pan oil on top! Then he put the eggs and sausage on the table near another plate piled high with black-eyed peas and poured half a cup of olive oil on *them*. Well, never mind, I thought. We were hungry, and ate heartily from the same common plates, washing everything down with homemade country wine he had poured into the two cloudy glasses.

With hunger and thirst satisfied, he started telling stories, how at the end of the First World War Greek soldiers returning from Germany had to get to Athens by any means possible. Many, like Barba Manolis, had to go most of the way on foot, a distance of some three hundred miles.

Then he married Maria, and they lived on the farm where he had lived as a child. His other brothers had left Greece to seek their fortunes – one to France, the other to the U.S. There were children – first a son, Yiorgos, then six daughters, and with them, six dowries to provide. Life was difficult, but when World War II exploded on the continent and both Italian and German troops occupied the island, it became precarious indeed. It was during this time that Maria became ill with tuberculosis and died. Manolis, then fifty, was left with seven children, the youngest three years old.

Survival was paramount. The occupying troops confiscated all livestock and produce. There was no soap and worse, no oil, except in the dead of night when contraband shipments arrived at remote beaches from larger neighboring islands. Manolis managed to secrete two or three sheep on the northern side of the island. Two of his younger daughters, then six and seven, tended them, sheltering themselves with the steaming animals in crude stone hovels. The eldest daughter, Marsó, traveled once a week out the dirt road in order to replenish their meager supply of bread and cheese, a few tomatoes. When these ran low, they survived on the rich sheep's milk alone.

After the war, his large brood still intact, Manolis cooked, cleaned, worked the farm and earned extra money as a stonemason on the side. They all survived at a time when starvation took many lives. And somehow, as the money came in, he purchased a field or a house in town, and in time provided a dowry for each of his six daughters. Once

I asked him why he had never remarried. He'd often thought about it, he told me, but hadn't done so for two important reasons: he knew there would be another large batch of children, and he was afraid that when they were all grown, the two factions would feud over property. And too, he had genuinely loved Maria; there could be no one to replace her.

Sometimes as the hour ripened and we sat sipping wine, the conversation blended into the realms of religion and spirituality. He often talked about the Bible stories he heard in church. Since he had never learned to read, his knowledge of the Bible had come from verses read in the Orthodox services every day – all visually aided by the numerous icons and paintings that adorned the church walls. His understanding of the New Testament parables was literal, and if he had any doubts that the events of Genesis occurred just as he was told in the scriptures, he never voiced them. He didn't make a big thing of it either, and simply accepted the parables in the manner they were offered.

I sat listening to the old tales of Adam and Eve, of Moses, Abraham and the prophets, of the Sower and the Seed and the Wise and Foolish Maidens – people who to him were not symbols, but who had been almost as real as I was sitting across from him. And for those brief moments, they came alive for me too, as their stories were passed on to me in the fresh voice of the original oral tradition. Uncluttered by learned theorizing, these had simply been live, flesh and blood people who had gone before us and who, through their own experiences, had been chosen by God to show those who came after how to live good lives.

"Have you lived a good life, Barba?" I asked him one night. He shrugged and pointed to the ceiling. God would judge.

At the end of these evenings he'd ask me to make the coffee. I'd get the copper *bríki* from the dish drainer and measure out the coffee and sugar and water as he directed. While the brew came to a boil, I stood at the stove behind him, keeping an eye on the contents of the *bríki*. Every once in a while I'd glance at the top of his slightly balding head as he sat quietly thinking, hands folded loosely in his lap. It was at those times that a strange warmth would catch me up and I realized how much I loved this old man. Later, I understood that the intense affection I had for him was the love for grandfathers I had never known – and for my father who had died when I was fifteen.

After coffee, when the time for departure approached, he filled a small sack with a few tomatoes, some onions, zucchini – whatever was in abundance and in season. Occasionally, he would slip in a bottle of that very special homemade wine. Always I left with burdens, happy ones, to carry up the hill and out the country road to my house.

* * *

I protest all the attention I am getting, Flora's time that I am taking, which already is overburdened with work. But no, she says, it is a small thing, they have so much, and I am their friend. I thank them, and before I can even begin to wonder how to get it all to my house on foot, she adds that her sixteen-year-old son, Manolis, will drive me and the huge bag to my gate two kilometers away on the back of his new Honda scooter.

Two days later I decide to visit some other friends in the country and stop at the farm on my way back. Visibly weaker, Barba Manolis is seated sideways on the bed, his back to the wall, while two of his daughters, Dina and Vangelo feed him something in a glass with a spoon. He had vomited all the previous day, they inform me; I am surprised that they are still trying to feed him. Finally he lies down. He seems glad to see me, and he says a few things, but his words are hard to understand, because his false teeth are out and he is very weak. Dina cries quietly on and off, and a roll of paper toweling is passed around. Flora, intent on her role as cook and keeper of the farm, comes in with a large plate of freshly-fried meatballs and passes them, demanding that each of us "eat, eat."

Marsó arrives in her son-in-law's taxi, with bundles. I take one and glance inside: the black lapel and blue and white striped dress shirt — Barba Manolis's burying clothes. Marsó enters the room. "How is he? No, you're not going to die, you're just sick, that's all," her voice a little hysterical with the effort of the lie she is trying to convince herself is true. "I'm going to die," he tells me. "I know, Barba," I say quietly. I am holding his hand, which is warm and dry. Marsó interrupts us, "No, you're not going to die — you will soon be up, and Anna will paint another portrait of you." The old man and I exchange glances. "Yes." I say. "I haven't forgotten. I am starting to paint it now." He says a few more words and then kisses me goodbye with the multiple, tender smacks the Greeks reserve for their small children. I want to say more, but haven't the words and get up to leave.

"Go with the good," he reminds me.

I hesitate. "And you," I respond, and he smiles. I leave the sickroom and the farm and set off down the road, noting the strange dampness in the air.

The next day, the south wind has begun to blow, an unusual phenomenon

*for August, when the prevailing wind is always dry and northerly. I go
to the carpenter and order a board cut in the shape of a small oval for
the portrait.*

* * *

One evening Barba Manolis had dropped by on his way back to town
and spent a good deal of time looking at my paintings stacked in corners and hanging on the walls. What all this uncharacteristic attention added up to was that he wanted me to do his portrait. At that
point, I had only been painting a short while, and had never once done
a portrait. But I accepted the challenge, and we struck a deal: for one
oil portrait, Barba Manolis would give me one month's free rent.

I needed about three one-hour sittings at a time of day when the
light was still good. Almost always busy in the mornings, he usually
came by about three o'clock, siesta time. For the first fifteen minutes
or so, he managed to stay pretty alert. But then he'd begin to nod off,
and I would have to whistle to perk him up again. After this happened
repeatedly, I realized he needed something to do, and I turned the
easel so he could monitor the progress of the work. This proved to
be a good solution, except for the disconcerting changes of expression, which I guess gauged his faith in the outcome. I forged ahead,
tryng to ignore this, grateful he was awake and his eyes were alert.

The portrait was completed, and it was a respectable job too, even
though his face was slightly too fat and the folds in his jacket a little
wooden. Barba Manolis was pleased, except for one small change he
wanted me to make: I hadn't gotten the curl in his moustache right,
But his moustache didn't curl, I protested, and went straight down
like a walrus's. He wanted it to curl anyway and demonstrated with
the hairs between thumb and forefinger just how much. Professionals
must sometimes have to sacrifice truth for vanity, I reasoned, and made
the small adjustment. Barba Manolis was happy, and maybe even proud,
for he hung it opposite his bed next to the armoire, where everyone
coming to visit couldn't help but see it and where it was the first thing
he saw, after St. George and the Blessed Virgin, upon waking in the
morning.

That was the first portrait, but not the last. I decided to do another
one for myself, and this one proved to be the better likeness of the
two. He wanted to buy this one as well, but I decided not to sell it
to him or to anyone else. "For me to remember you by," I told him,

and he seemed satisfied, maybe even a little flattered. I showed the portrait at the "Montparnasse," a fashionable bar/expo where I had my first exhibition on the island, and he came to the opening in his Sunday suit and sat by his portrait the entire evening, as the jet-setters awash in French perfume sailed through, so they would know who the distinguished-looking man in the portrait was and could compare the likeness.

One day he asked me to do a very small painting of him, so that when his family removed the bones from the graveyard four years after his death, there would be a color portrait instead of the usual fading black and white photograph hanging in the family chapel near the marble plaque sealing the niche where his bones would have their final rest.

*   *   *

I return home with the board for the portrait, and the day passes uneventfully until four, when an American friend comes by. He says he has just been to see Barba Manolis and suspects he won't last the night. The sixth daughter, Anna, has finally arrived from Athens on the three-thirty plane. Later, down at a cafe near the harbor, I sip an ouzo *as the sun goes down, and Costas, the owner, comes by the table to ask us if we'd heard the news, that Barba Manolis had died at four-thirty.*

Out at the farm later, the terrace is filled with people. All his daughters are gathered around the strangely small blue box, supported by two chairs. Inside, the corpse is wrapped in a white shroud, face hidden at sunset. I offer my condolences, and Dina tells me of his final moments, how her father had waited for the last daughter, Anna, to arrive. The two shared about a half hour together. Then he closed his eyes, and soon there were two or three sighs, and he was gone. With his last breath he had cried out for Maria, his wife, dead thirty-seven years. I listen with a curious detachment, nodding absently, unable to relate to the shrouded thing in the box.

The next afternoon I return to the farm to join the procession into town. The family and supporting women friends are gathered on one side of the coffin. On the other side, friends and neighbors come in and sit a few minutes to pay their respects and then depart for the terrace. Barba Manolis's granddaughter sits on the lap of her godmother. They both gaze sadly at the old man's face, which is unshrouded now, the body from chin down bowered in astors and chrysanthemums interspersed with large clumps of sweet basil. The room is filled with the smell of burning wax, basil and the sounds of sighing and weeping, that accompany the tender ministrations of Marsó, whose unofficial duty as eldest daughter and chief female mourner is to stimulate and direct the outpouring of grief.

A certain amount of theatrical finesse is necessary in this delicate task, for it is easy to go overboard into melodrama and stimulate hysteria, where hair is torn and clothing rent, acceptable behaviour when it is the untimely death of a young person, but in modern times somewhat out of place for this eighty-seven-year-old man. And so, Marsó sits stroking his head softly, calling up memories from years past.

I can't see his face — just the top of this head, where the sparce, gray hair is getting smoothed, disarranged and smoothed again in a gentle, continuous cycle by Marsó's work-roughened fingers. I can see just the top of his head, but it is enough to cause my tears to flow finally — hot, big drops that splash on the floor in spots the size of ten-drachma pieces. I have no chair, so I sit at the end of Barba Manolis's bed, which is covered from head to foot in a clean, white counterpane. No one objects or says anything, and it isn't until later that I learn I was probably seated on the feet of the dead man's spirit. Barba Manolis would have enjoyed it, I consoled myself later for the faux pas. And even if it had been uncomfortable — if spirits can be uncomfortable — I suspect that, in his great courtesy, he had solved the problem in a most unique way.

As I sit listening to the sighs and laments, the movement of a small object under the corner of his pillow catches my eye. I lean closer to see what it is and recognize the silvery shape of a moth nestled in the folds of the pillowcase. Perhaps Barba Manolis had indeed risen, I thought, succumbing to the fantasy, not in the glorious panoply of a colorful and majestic butterfly, but as a simple, gray moth tucked under the fold of pillow beneath the left ear of the body he had so recently deserted.

I leave the death chamber and walk into the fierce, white heat reflecting off the walls and terrace of the house. A steady stream of people arrives to pay last respects. Flora and Maria pass around cold water and sweet liqueur for the women, cognac for the men. The small parlor is filled with people trying to escape the sun. It is three o'clock, the hottest part of the day; everyone here, under ordinary circumstances, would be taking a siesta. We try to ignore the sweat. Barba Manolis's son Yiorgos stands pale and shy in his unaccustomed role as official greeter, responding with averted eyes to the countless "zoí sé sás" (life to you), the accepted expression of condolence.

When two priests arrive, the chairs are removed from the death chamber and final prayers at the house are chanted. The lid is placed on the coffin, and with five neighbors and his son acting as pall bearers, Barba Manolis is taken for the last time from the house where he was born and spent his childhood, where he raised his own seven children and where, after four *years, his bones will return for their final rest in the family chapel, to await the resurrection he had heard about from the scriptures.*

Vangelo, the daughter whose house I rented when I first met Barba Manolis, calls out in one tearful, melodramatic moment "Kaló Taxídi, Barba Manoli", " (Bon Voyage), verbalizing the thought of many of us, too prudent to say it ourselves. One of his granddaughters begins to cry and I hold her; I am comforted by being the comforter, as I give in to the overwhelming urge to touch and hold these people whose loss I share.

The short drive to town begins. The casket sits in the back of a neighbor's pickup with the black-clad figures of seven grown children surounding it, a dark tableau silhouetted against the relentless blaze of the sky. Two buses, numerous trucks and cars take us the ten-minute drive to the hill overlooking town. We disembark there and walk slowly in a long procession behind the small blue casket into the embrace of narrow, winding streets. It is nearly four, still siesta time, and the town is deserted. The few tourist shops that remain open quietly shut their doors out of respect. The church is filled, and we stand tightly packed and swaying against each other, steaming in the smell of incense, burning beeswax and sweat, as the ancient chants of the Liturgy for the Dead rise up above us to the dome, and reverberate against the immense icon of Jesus painted there, who gazes down in wisdom and compassion at the teeming, suffering creation.

I don't hear the liturgy, don't register it; I am still thinking and remembering. I stand facing the head of the casket, but a good distance back by the door. Still I haven't seen his dead face — only the top of his head; still the tears come, though gently now. I keep remenbering that view, the top of his head, when I had gotten up to make us coffee in the copper bríki at the end of those many meals I'd eaten in his rough little home — how as many times I had looked down at that head with love. How sad and unreal it is to be saying goodbye.

We move out into the fresher air of the square and assemble for the final procession to the cemetery. A bent and deaf woman of nearly a hundred years, who had been a neighbor of mine that first winter in the hóra, gives me a wide, toothless smile and asks if she can lean on my arm during the walk. I must bend down to her in order to support her, and by the time we reach the cemetery ten minutes later, I feel about ninety myself. But it is nice to be asked, to be so accepted, so cheered by that cavernous smile.

At the cemetery the coffin is uncovered one last time, one last look for the family, the final goodbye, and then the strange, high-topped black shoes are removed — shoes that have never walked the whitewashed streets of the town, shoes the dead wear, but are not buried in, on the celebration day of their last great rite of passage on earth.

Chapter Seven

Hierosphýia

> *"O dolphins of the barnyard, frolickers*
> *in the gray and eternal muck, in all your parts*
> *useful, because I have known you, this is the sage,*
> *and salt, the sacrificial markers of pepper.*
> *What pity should I feel, or gratitude, raising you*
> *on my fork as all the dead shall be risen?"*
> — Rodney Jones
> "For the Eating of Swine"

IT WAS EARLY NOVEMBER, AND EVERY YEAR AT THAT
time, in the land and its people, on farms and in villages all over Greece,
a quickening occurred, a little leap in activity after the brief rest following
the immense physical effort of the harvest. It started in October, really,
when the earth, parched all summer long to a dull gray, was drenched
by the first autumn rains. By late October the soil had darkened and
become swollen, ready by November to sprout the first delicate ten-
drils that would leaf out and blanket it in a fresh green counterpane.
The seasons seemed reversed here from my experience as a native of
the upper midwestern part of the United States. Life in Greece, green
life anyway, withered away in April and May to be reborn in October.

 With the dusty air of summer washed clean by the rains, it was time,
too, for the annual sprucing-up of barns and houses. While the men
slopped whitewash onto the dwelling's exterior, the women inside sorted
through boxes and drawers, setting aside the useful from the unuseful

out of what had been collected over the year. They wiped dust and dead flies off the high shelves and from under tables where the olive crocks and fifteen-kilo cans of oil were kept. They washed grit and char from lamp reservoirs and installed new wicks. When all surfaces were clean the men came in and whitewashed the interior walls and floors while the women, their backs bent over their task, vigorously scrubbed the tough and brightly woven wool of the striped dowry blankets. Then in the warm wind of midday, they draped them, secured by stones, so that the blankets flapped against the dry-stone walls like garlands of fall flowers.

In the villages and towns the *pantapolía* were busier than ever. Though there might be little or no choice of style or brand, as in all general stores, customers were sure to find at least one of anything they might need. They could buy a bar of green laundry soap or a wedge of cheese cut from a round two feet in diameter. Or have the proprietor measure a length of rope on a meter stick nailed to the counter. Or weigh a kilo of 5mm nails or a half kilo of patching putty on the same scale later used to weigh slabs of dried cod, stiff and pungent in their frost of brine.

It was not unusual to enter one of these stores in November and find it crowded with women, backed up against each other, pushing ahead, vying for a place next in turn. "Excuse me, I have work, I have work" echoed around the store as one or two women elbowed their way forward, as if no one else but they "had work" to do. It amused me how skillfully they accomplished their goal, greeting neighbors, relatives, gossiping as they smoothly edged forward. As one approached me the conversation followed the usual pattern:

"Ah, *yiá sōu*, Anna! How are you, good? Much rain (wind, heat, cold) we are having. Ah, poor me! My heart (my back, my legs) – how can I take this waiting when I have so much work to do!?" Then the smile and the nod and the not-so-gentle elbow nudging me out of the way, and she was one step – or one person – closer to her prize.

At first I was uncomfortable, but soon I grew to enjoy all this physical contact with strangers. It was liberating and even fun for me, the shy westerner, used to a wider sense of personal space and to the orderly lines of people in supermarkets who rarely talked to one another as they patiently waited their turns. It was amusing and fun unless, of course, I happened to be in a hurry too. Then, with a smile, I'd stand my ground, saying, "Sorry, but I too have work." Undaunted, she would be off to cluck with someone else in her path to the front of the line.

One brisk morning I ran into Eleni, the mother of my friend Andreaus from the north side of the island. She was calling orders to the clerk, a soft, pudgy man with Coke-bottle glasses. Eleni looked at me with a characteristic tilt of her head and wry smile as a woman near her pushed her way forward. "Well, what can we do? It's a busy time for everyone." She said. "We'll get through it slowly, slowly."

That could have been the one philosphy with which Eleni approached life – patiently, without hurry. Not that she had all the time in the world; she simply knew how to take the time necessary to complete a task. And not that she had so little work. In fact, her work had multiplied in the years since her husband Vassilis had died. Eleni simply did the best she could with the necessary chores. Beyond that, she didn't fret about getting anything perfect.

When the clerk returned with a ten kilo bag of sea salt, Eleni called off one-by-one the other items on her list: Five meters of plastic tablecloth – the one with the blue cornflowers intertwined in brown latticework – which he cut from the big bolt in a corner of the hardware room. And then came a kilo and a half of salt cod, a ten kilo can of oil, two kilos of olives and two of feta cheese, carved from the large, ripe hunk in a wooden barrel at the back of the store.

These were huge amounts; something was in the wind. "You will come to our *hierosphýia* on Friday?" she asked in Greek in the usual manner that always made invitations from them seem like demands. A *hierosphýia*, loosely translated, was a pork-eating party. It was also an all-day work marathon, beginning in the hours before dawn and ending nearly twenty-four hours later. I said that Andreaus had already invited me and that I was looking forward to being there.

"Could I come early and help?" I asked.

Eleni seemed impressed that a foreigner would offer to get up that early, not to mention actually volunteering to work. "So. You want to come early and kill the pig?" she asked, her head tilted and eyes sparkling in that wry smile. "Dimitri Lefkos is coming early from town. See if you can catch a ride with him."

*   *   *

If one thing was certain, it was the uncertainty at six or seven A.M. of my Greek alarm clock actually going off. That Friday morning, when I had to be up at 3:30, I particularly didn't want to risk keeping anyone waiting. Instead of the mechanical clock, I decided to depend on my inner alarm (the more reliable of the two, anyway) and was up and ready when Dimitri and his brother Lefteri arrived at my gate at four. They sandwiched me between them on Dimitri's huge BMW motor-cycle, and we began the slow meandering over the rough roads snaking through the silent, sleeping countryside. I have always loved being up at this hour – still a little groggy, as I was this morning, but acute to the fresh bite of the pre-dawn air, and to the low voices of the men, barely discernible from the rumble of the engine, as Dimitri maneuvered his load between ruts and around stones on the road leading to Eleni's farm. One other thing that was certain: it was going to be a very long day.

By the time we arrived at the farm Eleni and Andreaus had been up for an hour in order to feed the animals and start a cauldron of water heating over a fire in the barn. They greeted us in low voices, as if it were imperative we not disturb the sleep of the neighbors a quarter of a mile away.

Michalis and Panayiotis, neighbors from across the valley, and Costas, a friend of Andreaus from town, arrived to help. Eleni was dressed for work in an old gray dress with a black wimple tied over her hair. She invited the men in and offered us all coffee. We sat in the shadowy kitchen talking in hushed tones as we waited for the water to boil.

Eleni's kitchen was small for the eight of us, and not everyone had a seat. Coals smoldered in the raised corner fireplace near the door leading out to the freshly whitewashed terrace. Coffee began to rise up in a brown froth in the *bríki* on the three-burner gas plate. On the opposite side of the room, a cabinet with a curtain drawn across its front housed large jars and cans of staple items like oil and flour. In one corner a lumpy, narrow cot, covered in one of Andreaus's old army blankets, provided space at its foot, where Eleni sat having her meals alone from the small table in the adjoining corner.

*   *   *

I had met Eleni and her son Andreaus just a year and half before. One day shortly after we met, Eleni and I sat at the small table and ate from a large bunch of grapes on a plate. Almost crisp in their freshness, these grapes popped between my teeth as I listened while she told about her life.

She had grown up on the south side of the island near Aghios Yiorgos's Church. She had never attended school. As the eldest of fourteen children, she had to help care for the younger ones. As they progressed in school the small brothers and sisters taught her to read too, and even write a little. Then Vassilis came to court her. When they were married, she left her childhood home and came to live with him at his family farm in a wide valley on the north side of the island.

Eleni missed her first home very much. "Every evening as we were growing up, we could watch the sun setting behind the island of Delos. After I married and moved here, I never visited my family farm again. My brothers and sisters, they come here to see me. Life is, well, softer on the south side."

"Not so much work, you mean?" I asked.

"No, no, my child, I don't mean we didn't work as hard there as we do here — there is always work to do if you are a farmer."

I thought I understood what she meant, though. There was a difference in the atmosphere between the south and north sides of Mykonos. Occupied by the barite mine and long stretches of barren and precipitous shoreline, the sparcely settled northern coast received the brunt of the Meltemi, *the ferocious wind that blew for months, unhindered, all the way down from the Russian Steppe. Life was harsher there than on the south side, where the farms were protected by a ridge of high hills.*

Eleni first bore a daughter, Frascoula, and then remarkably, fifteen years later, Andreaus. Frascoula married a man from the main town, and Andreaus left school at twelve for Athens to apprentice in construction. Later, he joined the army, and while he was there, his father died.

Ten years later he returned to the island, and spent his days helping to build new hotels for the burgeoning tourist trade. Evenings he spent in cafes or tavernas *with friends, one of whom was our mutual friend Tom from the United States, who had bought some land near a beach. Andreaus had helped him negotiate the price and would soon begin building a house there. Since I still hadn't seen the land by the time Tom returned to the States, Andreaus offered to take me there.*

We had walked forty-five minutes from the nearest road over a rough, rock-strewn path before we finally came around a hill and saw the sea again. The site of the house was a small plateau about seventy meters in from the sea. A sand beach formed a necklace of white between the turquoise water and gray rocks rising above it.

We were hot and dusty from the motorcycle ride and the long walk from the road, and quickly stripped to our suits and dove into the calm sea. After the swim I unwrapped some cheese, a half loaf of brown bread and some fruit I had brought along in my knapsack. We ate, letting the juicy peaches and melon satisfy our thirst.

We talked about the house that would be built (one room with a sleeping platform, a fireplace and an indoor bathroom); who the master builder was going to be (a gray-haired friend he drank with named Manos); how it was going to be financed (Tom would send money from the States to a special account that Andreaus could draw out of); what work I did (painted); Walls? (pictures); what work he did (walls).

When we ran out of things to talk about, the silence stood between us like an invisible presence. We were out there, isolated from human habitation for miles around. We avoided each other's eyes and lay back, letting the sun, the breeze, the warm sand and soft lapping of the sea sink into our bodies.

I must have slept, because I woke up abruptly at the tentative touch of his hand on my bare arm. I opened my eyes. He was lying on his back looking at me. The intensity of the sun, the deep blue sky and sea, the stark, hot sand, were reflected in his eyes.

"Anna," was all he said.

Months passed, and our relationship bloomed. His family thought the sun itself had settled on their doorstep and hoped he would finally marry and build a new life for himself with the foreigner. Eleni looked forward to having a daughter-in-law to keep her company during the long winter evenings and to help her with chores that were beginning to overburden her fifty-six-year old body.

"Work." Eleni would say to me. "It's nothing but work. Much, much work, Annoula, living here on this farm. With the house alone, one woman could be busy all day."

While it was always clean enough, it was clear that Eleni couldn't keep up with the housework. Signs of neglect were reflected everywhere, in the piles of old clothes in corners, and shadows protruding from under one of the beds, hinting that old, dusty things were stored there. High up in the corner above where the two of us sat, a cobweb spanned nearly a foot at its widest point. It was covered with soot from the oil lamps and threatened to drop on the plate of grapes like a giant trap. Because of all the farm work she had, Eleni had been forced to give up the pride felt by most Greek women in their spotless houses, where bed linen was stripped and aired each day in the hot sun, floors were swept and washed (or whitewashed), where family treasures were dusted, arranged and rearranged like holy relics.

There was no time in Eleni's life for such luxuries as pride in keeping a spotless home. Everyday she was wakened before dawn by the old rooster in the yard. After whispering her morning prayers, she hastily dressed and went out to the darkened barn to feed the chickens and three donkeys. Then she hiked over several fields and rickety stone walls to where a small flock of sheep was grazing, and sat hunched on the damp ground, tugging at the ewe's teats, as the white stream squirted into the pail and a warm foam of butterfat rose slowly toward the rim.

Back at the house she skimmed off the butter and heated some of the milk for her breakfast, breaking thick rusks into it that expanded like tiny sponges. Up two hours, she had fed every creature on the farm that needed to be fed and finally had a chance to sit down and feed herself.

With the rest of the milk Eleni made cheese, a multi-stepped process involving not only that day's milk, but milk from two and three days past that had become cheese in various stages of readiness. Then there was the unending need for fresh water. And it was drawn and carried to the house without the aid of pump nor yoke nor strong man, for she had used the two pails of water Andreaus had drawn while she was milking, for the laundry. And laundry always seemed to be waiting, soaking in large pans out in the sun. After the scrubbing and rinsing came the tedious draping of each garment over the walls, where nature at last interceded and dried and half ironed it for her.

Yes, it was work living on such a farm. Eleni had been right: with the house alone, a woman could indeed be kept busy all day. As I write I try to remember. Had she said that with a meaningful nod of her head? Was the housework going to be my responsibility, then? Or would it be the farm? We never openly discussed it — the possibility of Andreaus and I marrying — but the prospect always seemed to be lurking in subtle corners of our times together.

And how did I feel about marrying her son? There were times, yes, when I thought that island was where I wanted to be and I wanted to be there with him. Those August days with the Meltemi *howling and I, sitting on a rock with his big, yellow dog, straining to hold sight of the fluorescent orange marking on Andreaus's snorkel far out in the heaving whitewater of the bay. He'd come in to shore, finally, a grouper or moray eel on the end of his spear gun, his face lit with quiet excitement and pride. Or the time he saved the life of one of his ewes when he took one of her inflamed and filthy teats into his mouth and blew hard to dislodge whatever was blocking her flow of milk. Or camping on a deserted beach, when we pretended we were shipwrecked, and he shot a rabbit for our supper, and we swam naked in the moonlight, the sea dancing with phosphorous, then waking at dawn to find a viper snoozing beside us in the crevice of a rock.*

And Andreaus: dark, curly hair, eyes, sensitive and intelligent, but with the hint or shadow of some secret fear he seemed to forget with a whiskey or two. Gentle. A dreamer's heart beneath the powerful muscles he'd developed in the labor of his work.

He provided the gateway into a life that was stocked constantly by primal things: the smells of wild oregano and thyme, the harsh, rocky soil, so barren that I wondered how it could ever support life, exploding in a lush canopy of green in October and a whole palette of wildflowers. The births, deaths, and celebrations, the sharing of labor and sorrow and joy that comes with life lived in a small place like an island, whose perimeters were distinct, and whose codes of honor and sense of community were intertwined in a generosity and tolerance that couldn't be measured. Yes, life was harsh there, but it could also be incredibly sweet.

But when Andreaus and I finally got around to talking about marriage, we both had doubts that our lives could blend in a harmonious way. Because of my artistic interests I was too sensitive, he said, for the life of a Greek farm wife. He didn't like the idea of marriage anyway. "A gilded cage," he called it. And I, the "sensitive artist" I was at the time, tended to agree. Still, we went on.

*   *   *

At last the cauldron of water in the barn had begun to boil. Dimitri sat honing his knives and other butchering utensils. He was known for his skill in slaughtering animals and kept the knives carefully wrapped in a piece of chamois, slipped into a steel cylinder and closed with a shiny brass cover. He had asked the local blacksmith to make this container and was very proud of the craftsmanship. The smithy had sealed its joints with brass and crimped the edges in a decorative pattern. Dimitri recognized the same regard for craftsmanship in this container that he had once given to his work in construction, to the pigs' lives he had ended with speed and as little pain as possible – and to the occasional feminine conquest for which he was known as well. In his fifties, and not a large man, he possessed the kind of sinewy strength of so many who labor daily with their backs and arms and hands. Dimitri, a swaggering, moustachioed man, a Lothario with an irrepressible roving eye. His comely wife, Chrisoula, had been enduring with equanimity her husband's licentiousness for nearly thirty years. He would have been devastated without her.

The water was hot; the knives were as sharp as they were going to get. The men walked out together to the side of the barn just as Andreaus guided the pink and brown spotted sow out of her pen and prodded her into the clearing. She swung her head back and forth in what seemed to me to be nervousness. What was this unaccustomed intrusion into her morning habits? I imagined her thinking. Where was her breakfast, and why had she no dinner the night before? Who were all these men, their voices low and tense, their eyes on her?

Once she reached the clearing near the barn, the men positioned themselves one at each foot and another at her head. At Dimitri's signal they upended the struggling pig onto her back. I wanted to turn from the view as her screams sliced through the cold morning air. For a brief moment I felt numb, as if some grotesque rape were taking place. I didn't want to watch what I knew came next, but forced myself to do so, trying in vain to switch to the mind of an anthropologist.

Dimitri's skill ended all our miseries very quickly. Straddling the screaming pig, he quickly traced the sign of the Cross on her upturned chest with his stiletto, before carefully positioning its tip and poking a hole through the thick hide of her throat. Switching to the double-bladed dagger, he deftly and in one swift stroke severed both her spinal column and main artery. The whole thing was over in less than a minute. The pig's screams stopped abruptly, leaving the countryside suddenly silent. Her great hulk relaxed, all that energy suddenly useless, diffused and colliding in unseen molecules in the shivering air. The momentary silence was broken as the two dogs, cowed earlier by the chaos of the thrashing pig and shouts of the men, made a beeline for the fresh blood pouring out of the wound, lapping it up off the dust of the barnyard, yelping and trembling with excitement.

Our moods lightened once the actual slaughter was accomplished. Andreaus and Lefteris brought buckets of boiling water from the cauldron to pour over the carcass. "Carcass," I called it. Now it was no longer a pig, but a "carcass." "It" was now in that odd and indeterminate state between being alive and being food for something else alive. "Food," what the carcass would be as soon as it was butchered and cooked – or more precisely, "pork." Or "*hierinó*," as the Greeks called it.

I watched as hot water loosened the bristles so the men could scrape them off easily with their sharp pocket knives, and I wondered if they ever thought of this moment as they stood before their shaving mirrors. As Dimitri slowly poured the water, the others worked their way down the length of the carcass, clouds of steam and the smell of blood enveloping them. Dimitri called to his wife, who had just arrived by taxi, to bring out the razors and fresh blades. Then he, Andreaus and

Lefteris took over, carefully shaving the last of the stubble down to the finely grained hide.

When the bristles were removed, the hard work began. With a pulley they hoisted the carcass by its hind feet onto a beam securely anchored high into the wall of the barn. Dimitri took a large butchering knife and removed the head, reserving from the neck a large chunk of tender meat to place on the brazier. He opened up the abdomen from the anus to the ribcage and spread open the flaps of hide and fat, exposing the internal organs. I stepped closer in order to see better.

What I had expected to see didn't match what was there: all the finely shaped organs fitted together so perfectly. And how clean and orderly it was, like a fancy gift box of cheeses and salami that one orders from ads in the back of *Town and Country*.

I had studied biology and zoology in college, had cut up frogs, cats and, yes, even a fetal pig. But for some reason I expected the filth and mess of a pig's exterior life to be reflected in its interior. After all, the fetal pig of college days had come to the dissecting tray directly from that universally sacrosanct state, *in utero*, connoting a kind of pristine innocence, trust and above all, purity. The other organs I could only assume would accurately reflect the rest of the adult pig – and all pigs, including the one we'd just dispatched, who had spent many of her living hours lying with all her incredible bulk in mud and slop, nose dripping as she snorted in wise mistrust, perusing the world about her with pale blue eyes fringed in long, blond lashes.

But even when the residue of excrement escaped from the withdrawn intestines (mostly purged after a twelve-hour fast), I noticed it was as unrepulsive as a newborn babe's.

Perhaps I had been too hard on mud and pigs after all. Perhaps it was only in cities (my thoughts rushed on), in cities so remote it seemed from the natural cleansing forces of wind and rain, only in cities that I would find real filth; that people in crowded cities – Athens no less than New York – were forced to live in their own filth (like the broken glass, empty syringes and used condoms one saw as a matter of course on the streets of the world's largest metropolises); that there really was no filth in the countryside outside large cities, but that everything found its place and purpose within the natural cycle; that there was nothing in nature to be repulsed by; and that everything in nature, including people and in spite of people in crowded cities, was good.

Well. Then even killing this pig (my reason leaping to greater and greater heights), causing it to change into food for the winter ahead, must also be good and as it should be. For we were all of us a part of nature and all nature preyed upon itself.

Perusing the world with wise mistrust, perhaps. But, until the moment that she was led out to the barnyard, I believe this pig never suspected that those who fed her and cared for her needs did so only that she should at some time be taken into their bodies, her parts becoming their parts. And just because the pig was mercifully ignorant of her fate didn't mean that this wasn't going to happen; it would indeed die and become food for some other, though not perhaps as some say, "higher" form of life. And if that were the case with the ignorant pig, and granting that the whole of nature preyed upon itself . . . who or what, then, would be eating . . . us?

Eleni interrupted my reveries by announcing breakfast. Out to the barnyard she came with forks in one hand and a platter of fried pork liver and bits of choice neck meat from the brazier in the other. We ate standing, spearing meat from the common dish and sopping up the hot fat with hunks of thickly sliced bread, washed down with the first tapping of the year's wine. Though it was only seven thirty, this unusual breakfast was delicious and revived our energy with its concentrated injection of calories.

The pace picked up again as everyone got back to work – the women to the kitchen to prepare the noon meal, the men to stripping the meat and lard from the carcass.

Two neighbor girls, Angeliki and Irini, arrived to help. Their job was to wash the intestines. They poured warm water three times through the meter-long lengths of small intestine, alternating with salt and lemon juice scrubs. By the time they were through, the intestines were clean and fresh-smelling enough to become the casings for the *lukániko*, or sausage.

I checked with Frascoula on what needed to be done. She gave me some tweezers and demonstrated how to remove the transparent membrane clinging to the pig's brain and covering a network of fine, gray nerves running through it. Meanwhile, Costas and Panayiotis cut the strips of lard into squares and rubbed each one in coarse sea salt. The corrosive action of the salt had reddened their already work-roughened hands, I noticed, as they placed the lard in crocks where it would be preserved the entire winter.

Outside, Dimitri was separating meat from the carcass and putting it in a large wooden tub, where Michalis and Lefteris cut it into coarse chunks. After he extracted the two tenderloins, Dimitri rubbed them with salt, pepper, oregano and thyme and with Andreaus's help, stuffed them into the large intestine. After the *loūza* had cured a month or so, this spicy "Canadian Bacon" would be sliced and eaten with *ouzo* or wine as a great delicacy.

I helped as much as I could washing dishes, fetching water and other such unskilled labor. By noon we were all tired and hungry. Eleni and the other women had made a succulent stew from the pig's stomach, all cut up with bits of heart and lung, braced with garlic and a generous amount of small, whole onions. The table was covered with plates of freshly fried liver, slabs of feta and mounds of shredded lettuce, sprinkled with fresh dill, lemon, and oil. On one plate, crisped to a golden brown and garnished with the ubiquitous lemon quarter was the pig's brain. We dug into the food like hungry pigs ourselves, and the table reeled with pandemonium as jokes flew back and forth and the new wine splashed into small glasses.

But everyone knew the real revelry would be saved for that evening. After the long morning's work and filled bellies, it was time for a siesta – for the men, anyway. They had finished their work for the day, unless they went off to their regular jobs, as a few did. The women wouldn't quit until after midnight. Not only did they have to prepare another and bigger evening meal, but they had to make the *lukániko*. The huge mound of cut up meat in the wooden tub testified to hours of labor ahead.

It was hard not to notice what seemed superficially to be a vast imbalance in the division of labor between men's and women's workloads. No matter how much work there was at these affairs, the men never helped if it in any way spoke of being "women's work." Women, on the other hand, were expected to do all the work of keeping the home, raising the children, cooking meals, plus helping out in the fields during planting and harvest. Lines indicating the division of labor were strictly drawn in the case of the man – he was provider, builder, protector, boss. But the woman's role, no less important than the man's as far as family survival was concerned, still seemed slightly blurred at its edges. Thus, women were also expected to contribute to the family income by spinning yarn or knitting sweaters to be sold in town to the tourists. They usually did this at night when all other work was done. When the men's jobs were finished they retired to the *tavernas* to relax with friends over a bottle of *retzina*.

Though they were always complaining about work, the women seemed content enough in their roles. Even though what they complained of came with the role they played, I had yet to meet a farm woman who suffered from low self-esteem.

When I spoke about this with my friend, Popie Marinou Mohring, an Athenian émigré to the United States, she pointed out that women's work was the same all over the world. "But we women are strong," she added, "strong in a different way than men. Men are strong like the *Voriás* (north wind). When it blows, it can uproot big and strong trees. But their *psychoúla* (little psyche) hangs like a cocoon from its silk thread."

In light of all this, I was surprised when Dimitri invaded the female domain of sausage making and insisted on taking responsibility for its seasoning. For two hours the women had been slicing up chunks of meat into the finest of slivers, using two very sharp knives, crossed as if they were cutting pastry. With a flourish, Dimitri rolled up his sleeves and took the plastic bag full of sea salt.

"Well, how much salt should I put in?" he half asked, half challenged, full hand extended and standing above the trough as several hours earlier he had stood over the struggling pig. "How much, how much do you say!" He scattered salt over the meat until it was covered in a fine white dust.

"More!" The onlookers all agreed, but on how much more they were divided. So Dimitri threw on a second, third and almost a fourth handful, until the congregation yelled in one voice, "Stop!"

"You want me to stop?" he teased with one eyebrow raised like some half-crazed priest.

Everyone was involved now, the remaining men, the children, even the cat who paced, tail high, meowing. Dimitri dropped the bag of salt and took the pepper. He was warming to his role as center of attention, and went through the same procedure with libations of pepper, thyme, oregano and sage. Even though his antics were getting a bit old, his captive audience dared not leave him in the midst of this very important process. When the seasonings had all been added in the proper amounts, Dimitri bent down and mixed them thoroughly with the meat. As the aroma of the raw mixture rose up like a fragrant mist and filled the room, everyone agreed it would be good; the *lukániko* would be good that year.

Recently more and more families had been buying the combination meat grinder/sausage stuffer that was attached to the edge of the table. It was amazing to me that here in the late twentieth century such a simple contraption should have been considered modern, since my great-grandmother had probably used one a century ago on the Canadian prairie. But many families like this one, living much as my ancestors had lived, had as yet no such device as a meat grinder/stuffer and continued to cut and stuff sausage in the old way.

Angeliki and Irini took the tin, funnel-like tools and stuffed the slivered, seasoned meat into the attached casing, pushing with their thumbs and letting the meter-long lengths slowly pan out. When a length was full, Frascoula held it high at its mid-point while Eleni looped it off into links, all the time measuring with her eye so that it came out even at the end. My job was to poke the links several times with a needle to release air. Then we took the *lukániko* out and hung it on the clothesline where it would dry a few days in the sun and wind. One of the men built a small fire for open air smoking – and for shooing away the flies.

There had been so much work so far for everyone that only the smallest children escaped. But learning was through the senses here, and less so from books, and even though the smallest participants had nothing to do but play, they still were absorbing information about their future roles through the sensual data provided them: sights, sounds and smells, the quiet security of the men telling stories as they rubbed salt into slabs of lard, that rhythmic soft shriek of metal against metal as the women sliced meat for the *lukániko*. As the children grew and it became time for them to contribute in more concrete ways, it was all there, collected in their unconscious, waiting to be tapped and used.

And I, too, was learning. My own senses, dormant from too much city living and bookish pursuits, came alive in this land of contrasts and absorbed countless new impressions and lessons. I watched and participated, assimilating it all, so that days later I might write about it in a letter to a friend. And years hence, it would bubble up from my memory in fresh images, fermenting like the year's grape pressing, to become new wine.

I went out to the terrace to help Eleni's two granddaughters clean a bushel of kale. Added later to the cauldron out in the barn, its flavor would blend with those others bubbling away at the star of the evening's celebration: the pig's head. Earlier, this head had been washed and shaven, had its ears cleaned and teeth brushed thoroughly by Andreaus and, for four hours or so, would stew all cut up in the iron cauldron.

At four I left to flag down a ride on the bus from Ano Mera and went home to rest a little and clean up before the festivities later at the farm. My clothes, hair, everything about me was saturated with the smell of fat. The idea of returning a few hours later to eat more "pig" almost made me nauseated. I went to the well and drew two big buckets of water to heat for a shampoo and bath.

My house was cold and damp inside from being closed up all day, so I collected some wood from the barn and built a fire in the kitchen fireplace. The wind was right, I noticed; the primitive chimney would draw well and not smoke.

I added some hot water to the cold remaining in one of the pails and carried it to the terrace to wash my hair. The last vestige of the thinning autumn sun barely warmed me, and the water had almost cooled by the time I finished. When water from the second bucket was hot, I got the yellow plastic bathtub from the studio and put it in the kitchen, pouring in the hot water that had been heating on the stove. I stripped down and sank into the warm water.

It steamed like dry ice into the cooler kitchen, fogging the cold windows that sucked out heat from the fire. My skin was thirsty for water; I could feel it drinking it in. I sat in this steamy room like some Stone Age cave dweller, watching the flickering firelight on its curved, white walls and wondered if I dared forego the feasting later on. It was so pleasant to be relaxing in this warm bath, the comforting firelight, peaceful, away from the pandemonium of the day's preparations. But I could enjoy the soak only a few minutes before it began to cool. I soaped down quickly and rinsed as best I could in the bubbly water and then rubbed down with a towel in front of the fire.

I felt a strong temptation to stay home, though I knew Eleni and Andreaus wouldn't understand my momentary need to withdraw, to be quiet, to sink into the warm womb of my house.

But I wanted to go to the party too. I wanted to be with them, to laugh and joke and eat until my sides burst. And besides, warm and cozy as my kitchen was at that moment, I knew the room on the other side of the door was cold, that the fire's heat was blocked by the closed door, and that once out of the tub, out of the kitchen and into the air of that room, I would not want to linger very long.

By the time I returned to the farm, several guests had already arrived and were seated around the long table Frascoula and Eleni had set up while I was away. Pandelis, a neighbor accompanied by his wife and granddaughter, Andreaus's aunt and uncle from across the valley, and Dimitri and Chrisoula – all freshly bathed and changed – were grouped around the table, talking, just as Iraklis and I arrived together. A year later Iraklis would return to Lesbos, his native island, but for now, he was a close neighbor, a vegetarian, which is why he hadn't participated in the day's work. But since he was practically a member of the family, he was, of course, invited to the party afterward.

When everyone had arrived, Eleni started filling plates from the contents of the cauldron that Andreaus and Costas had carried into the kitchen. In front of each person Frascoula set a plate of greens and a thick slice of boiled lard. Soul food. My own plate arrived, however, with an additional treat. I looked at Pandelis, the gnarled old farmer across from me.

"Eat," he said. "It is an honor to receive one." I looked down at it in my plate, poached white like an egg, faintly blue where the iris would be. The thought of eating an eye! And after a day of roiling around in pig fat!

I remembered one of Salvador Dali's experimental films of the thirties where a man sliced a straightedge razor through what appeared to be the eye of a beautiful young woman. In a deft slight-of-hand and camera, however, Dali had switched the human eye to a dead animal's. After my initial revulsion at seeing the vitreous humor squirt out of the sliced eye, I experienced an almost primal anger at Dali for treading, even in the imagination, into that tabooed area—the mutilation of the human eye, window of the soul.

I also remembered an icon of St. Lucia in the Catholic Church down in the *hóra*—Lucia, patron saint of light and, by extension, sight, standing placidly with two eyes staring up at her from a golden plate. Couldn't I demur and claim my fragile western sensibilities, as I had seen tourists do in similar situations? No. Though a foreigner, I was no tourist. Nor was I a saint, but I was still going to have to perform a miracle. I had to think of something else. I had to think of . . . chocolate covered cherries! I could do that, I thought, imagining the bittersweet mix of chocolate and drippy nougat, the spicy, almost crisp skin of the cherry. Yes, I could eat a chocolate covered cherry, chocolate covered cherry, chocolate covered . . .

I looked up at Dimitri, who had been "honored" with the other eye. He winked at me, speared the eye with his fork, put it in his mouth and proceeded to chew and chew and chew until I couldn't watch him any longer. Chocolate covered cherry, chocolate covered cherry . . .

Before I had time to think any more about it, I gingerly nudged the eye onto my fork (spearing it was out of the question). It was tough, judging from Dimitri's endless chewing, which was definitely a prospect I wished to avoid. So I closed my eyes and, like the giant anaconda of the Brazilian rain forest, swallowed the thing whole. Everyone applauded; it was indeed a great moment. The eye tasted like pork (for some reason this surprised me) and lay in my stomach like a stone.

Once everyone was served, we all embarked on a period of very serious eating for about a half hour. Then some less serious drinking, followed by more eating – mostly dipping into the small plates of fried cod, meatballs, salads and cheeses placed down the center of the long table. We helped ourselves with our forks from the common plates as was the custom, the idea of germs or cholesterol never entering anyone's head.

As the evening progressed, the *kéfi* began to rise. This was one of the first Greek words I learned, after "hello," "goodbye," "thank you" and a few words of profanity always slipped to the novice. My Greek/English dictionary approaches, but doesn't do it justice when it describes *kéfi* as "a good feeling, gaiety, merry, mellow." All these terms apply, all are true, but they are only a part of what I understood it to be. For me, and I think there are many who would agree, it is stimulated by music more than anything else – especially Greek (or Latin American) music with its peculiar effect on the solar plexus. It has to do with wine, of course, usually *retzina* and the slow, subtle progression of its effect. But even more, it has to do with the company, the smiles, voices singing – *kéfi* is the meeting of eyes in recognition that yes, this is a rare moment; that it's not just you, but I, too, am being carried away by this moment.

Waiting for *kéfi* to build at a Greek party was like waiting for a dynamite fuse to blow, but without the anxiety of destruction. Once hunger and thirst had been satisfied, if that were to be the end of it, the slowly building *kéfi* would have fizzled out like the pig's bladder Dimitri had earlier blown up for the children to play with. Instead, a very simple thing happened: the musicians would push back from the table, bring out their instruments – and begin to play.

In our case that night, someone put a record on an old battery-powered phonograph. The teenagers were first to get up to dance, tentatively at first. But soon their bodies became fluid, and their faces flushed with pleasure in the movements of the old dance and of having a chance at last to actually touch their sweethearts. They rested extended arms on the shoulders of their neighbors and danced in a circle with a heavy grace, as the young man at the end dipped and turned on one foot, just managing to keep his balance with help from the steady hand of the youth to his right.

With the next song, the rest of us got up to dance. My *kéfi* was high, and if I had ever been shy about dancing, it wasn't now, as I gave in to the oriental wail of the singer weaving rhythmically in and around the intricate embroidery of the *bouzoūki*.

Next came the slow, passionate music of the *Zembékiko*. Andreaus got up to dance this solo for men. Slowly he balanced the subtle steps, improvising as he went, bending, shuffling in the perpetual rhythm between the loss and regaining of balance so typical of this dance. Shy and hesitant at first at being the center of attention, he soon gave in to the music, back straight, eyes lowered, smoldering cigarette in his lips. Someone handed him a half-filled glass of wine, and he danced with it balanced on his head. Everyone called " '*Óh-pah!* '*Óh-pah!* " when it nearly spilled. His friend Costas hunkered down and clapped in time. Iraklis, in a burlesque moment of high *kéfi*, tossed a lemon wedge instead of the customary plate. But it soared too high and connected with the glass, knocking it off – an insult coming from anyone else but Iraklis, Andreaus told me later. The dancing and hilarity went on for another couple of hours, the room reeling in the bright glare of the gas lantern and endless cigarette smoke.

As the food, the wine and dancing began to catch up with us, the revelry quieted, and several who lived back in the *hóra* got up to leave. Soon there were just a few neighbors left. I remained as well, for Eleni and Andreaus had earlier invited me to stay the night.

I listened to the small talk, stories and reminiscences. Warmth. Eleni and Frascoula made coffee, an excuse to linger for the rest of us who were not eager for the evening to end – even though several of us had been up since 3:30 that morning. This quietness, compared to the boisterous fun of the previous three hours, created a kind of tension: another dynamite fuse about to go. But this one was more like a great swelling open of the hibiscus in June.

Someone started to sing – slowly, with characteristic oriental lilt – an old song, "maybe fifty years old," Andreaus whispered to me. Then Anna, a woman down at the other end of the table, chimed in an octave above. Before long the whole table had heaved itself up in a second wind and become a song.

I didn't know the words, but I could hum along. When that song was finished, Andreaus's uncle began another one about the *hierosphýia*, a multi-versed simple melody that celebrated the healthy pig, a full larder for the winter, plump links of *lukániko* and, most of all, the good company around the table that evening. Andreaus' uncle sang the first line and we repeated it in chorus.

Everyone knew this song; it had been handed down and added to for generations, and this fact made it even more poignant when I saw the daughter of an old friend leaning a little toward her husband as her eyes filled with tears. Her father, Barba Manolis, had died just over a year ago, and I too remembered how he had led that same song at another *hierosphýia* just before he died. We surrounded this woman in a swell of song, full-voiced, smiles lighting our faces and eventually even the face of the daughter through her tears.

As the verses faded, someone started yet another song. It was Eleni. She had been known in her youth for her beautiful singing voice. As with the previous song, she led off and the rest of us responded in antiphonal chorus. The sound of her voice, cracking a bit with age, was unhurried, passionate still. I remembered my small tape recorder back in the studio and wished I had thought to bring it. Like the old mountain singers of Appalachia, this voice too should have been preserved.

*   *   *

Eleni. I had only known her for a year and a half. There was soon to come a time when I would realize that I loved her even more than I loved her son. I spent many hours at their small farm — much time, in fact, becoming acquainted not only with her, but with her life, for there was that unspoken possibility lurking in the minds of all of us that Eleni's life could become mine as well. We baked bread together.

One morning, very early, I caught the bus and went out to the farm. Eleni had already mixed up the leaven the night before and had just added it to a large mound of flour in the wooden bread trough. In an hour this dough had swollen, filling the trough and causing the fragrance of warm yeast to fill the house. We rolled up our sleeves and sank arms up to elbows into the sticky dough, heaving its live weight around and under itself before forcing it down with the heels of our hands. Small bubbles puffed out more fragrance as they burst, and the dough became more and more elastic. Eleni demonstrated how to form the dough into rounds or into long slabs that we indented with a wedge-like knife all down their lengths. Broken apart after baking and dried out overnight in the dying heat of the oven, these rusks would be eaten for months, softened in water, or soup or milk long after her fresh bread had been consumed.

Whether it was fresh or dried, Eleni's was good, heavy, dark bread, punctuated by an occasional bit of straw or seed casing. It was a rough, full-wheat-flavored bread. A primal bread, baked by first farmers over open fires. I could imagine the earth it sprang from and the sun drawing it out of that earth, onto the threshing floor and through the grindstones, into Eleni's kitchen where it fed us, nourished us, where coarse clods of earth were transformed into food for us. It was almost sacramental, eating Eleni's bread.

I had to admit that I felt a tremendous attraction to her life. I thought of how it would be, leading a life close to nature with hard, simple work, life and death work sometimes. But I could also see my face and hands years ahead, reddened by weather like Eleni's, my fingernails encrusted with the harsh, stony soil. But more disturbing to me than these vain concerns, I could see myself spending long winter evenings after Eleni had died, sitting alone or with neighbor women, while our men were out in the tavernas. We would be knitting or spinning, talking about our sore backs, our husbands or speculating on whether St. Patapios would make an appearance at the vigil on the eve of his nameday. And when, in the midst of all this, would I ever find the time or energy or heart to pick up a paintbrush and paint a picture? Wouldn't my thirty years' experience in another environment count for anything here? Would I really have to think like a Greek, become Greek? At the time it seemed so, particularly because of Andreaus.

Of all the Greek men on the island who had married foreign women, and there were many, if he were to marry one, Andreaus was the man least interested in going to the United States. He was emotionally rooted in his homeland and had little respect for those who left to make money elsewhere, especially those who returned to the island speaking Greek laced with foreign slang and, like preening peacocks, showed off their new wealth. He never wanted to be like them. He would always be Greek, pure and incorruptible. In the end, it was the ambivalent feelings we both had about marriage to each other that proved stronger than our personal needs for companionship and intimacy and the plans of his relatives, clamoring for him to settle down.

Still, I loved my life here. Who could not love a lifestyle that, however difficult, was in a place of such breathcatching beauty? But even more important, I think I loved the life because each day brought me, the foreigner, something new to do, or see, or contemplate.

In fact, these were years of many firsts. I enjoyed the rhythmic bending and lifting of harvest, because I had never done it before, never worked so hard physically, never appreciated food so much or a hard mattress so thoroughly as I did after a day spent in a field helping Andreaus and his family cut and bind wheat. I loved life here, because it was so much more vivid physically than my life had been so far. Life and death were not abstractions on this island, but daily confrontations. Even the rain seemed wetter.

But was it as vivid to those who lived here? Did their life become old and ordinary to my Greek neighbors, as mine in the city had become for me? Eleni certainly didn't exhibit any great enthusiasm — only dogged persistence in her labor and a patient acceptance of the unchanging events of each day. And one young woman I knew longed to marry an Athenian to escape the work of the farm. As island suitors one after another proposed and were turned down, her resolve strengthened to escape a destiny of unending toil. But the Athenian knight never arrived, and her beauty faded in the years of caring for the farm and her aging parents.

Then there was my young neighbor who liked to draw and who wanted to study art in Athens. She used to come by to show me her drawings. But her parents had rarely been off the island and thought life here would be just fine for their only child. On walks I would pass by their farm and see her in the pen where they kept the two cows in winter. Shoveling out manure, she was docile as the cows, resigned to her future.

It did get old, the life here — especially for the young men who, after army duty, were returning in fewer and fewer numbers to the farms, preferring instead to seek work in Australia, South Africa or the United States. Mostly, it was old men who returned, to spend their final years in the place of their childhood, to rest at last in the intimate, stony soil of their native land.

So perhaps life here was so vivid to me, because, even after several years each day still yielded its newness. And its fleeting power was made clearer yet in the knowledge that any time I chose to, I was free to leave.

Were there times when my life before Greece had been equally vivid? I could remember the warm fecundity of a spring afternoon when I was five, picking wild violets for Mother's Day from the empty lot near our house. And when I was thirteen, the taste of my first cup of coffee and cream from a thermos with my father when we had stopped for lunch two miles up Spruce Creek, where we had gone to fish for brook trout. And I could remember the light and the sound of Canada geese on a still lake, or the virgin silence and smells at four in the morning as I crunched through the snow to meet friends for a ski trip.

But these were impressions from youth, and in youth everything is new and vivid. Perhaps that was why the old men returned: the vividness of the past brought suddenly alive and relived, replacing temporarily, and then only in their imaginations, the dry husk of their decline with

dewy memories of an unlimited horizon. So was it only a question of place,
then, or could there be something more, a particular innocence of seeing,
perhaps? Maybe I had fallen asleep with my eighteenth birthday, and
Greece had simply wakened me up again.

Rather than it being only a matter of place, what seemed the crucial
issue for me was the necessity of staying awake.

*   *   *

I looked at these people around the table, and I was vividly aware that I could be with them and love them and learn from them. But I realized with a painful, wrenching sadness, that I could never *become* them. I sat at Eleni's table, listening to her sing. I knew I was in the company of friends; I felt enfolded in the warmth and closeness of the moment. But I knew at the same time with a curious sense of conclusion, as if a door were finally – and very gently – being closed, that I would some-day leave this place.

The party began to break up. Pandelis stretched, and his wife nudged the grandchild's sleeping head resting in her lap. It was one in the morning. When everyone had left, I crawled in beside the two grand-daughters in the big bed on the balcony. We left the cleaning up until morning, but we all knew Eleni would rise at five and have it half done by the time the rest of us stirred.

Through the thin partition on the balcony I could hear her say her evening prayers in front of the family icons decked out on a shelf above her bed. I had long ago taken in all that rested on that shelf: the painted images on wood of the Virgin and Child and another of St. George slaying the dragon. Between them, a small bottle of holy water from the shrine at Tinos. And last, the glassed-in wooden box displaying the two crowns of white flowers from her wedding day, linked by a single white ribbon symbolizing the martyrdom of marriage.

In the midst of Eleni's prayers, in which I heard no words, only the soft rustle of whispers from behind the partition, I slept.

Chapter Eight
Theophilos

"O harsh surrounding cloud that
will not free my soul!"
— Walt Whitman

HE WAS CLOSE TO EIGHTY AND HEALTHY WHEN I MET him for the first time at his shop on one of the main streets of town. He sold yarn there, as well as string for fishermen's nets, and wholesale cigarettes. It was October, and he was seated in the sun outside the door of his shop, winding twine for goat hobbles through his long, still strong fingers. He wore an old gray sweater over a blue work shirt and baggy, dull green trousers. The blue visored hat all island men wore was pulled down over his brow at a rakish angle.

"*Yiá Sōu*, Kopélla," he greeted me in Greek with that tone of unmistakable invitation that Mediterranean men seem to possess regardless of their age.

"Hello, and how are you?" I smiled.

"I am fine." he answered slowly in his gruff voice. "Where you from, Ameriki? How long you stay?" The inevitable questions familiar to all tourists, everywhere.

We chatted a while, but I didn't linger; I had many errands and then the long walk up the hill. "You must go? Well, come and sit again another time."

I promised I would. And did so, many times.

*   *   *

If you were nicknamed "'Ákros," you were a man who lived the extremes. You ate, drank, fought and made love to the limits of your stamina and then beyond. Another person would think twice before provoking you if your nickname were "'Ákros."

Theophilos's given name meant "friend of God." But Theophilos, the quintessential macho man, was known from his tumultuous youth as "'Ákros."

It was well known that during the war when the Italians occupied the island, Theophilos had been a collaborator. The enemy had confiscated for their own use all livestock, bread, oil, vegetables – even soap – that the farmers produced. People were starving, especially in the *hóra*, where the tools of survival were attuned more to commerce than to land. Theophilos had a family to support, after all. But nearly every man those days had a family to support and, while he was not by any means alone in his betrayal, it was true that others had survived this dark hour in Greece without collaborating with the enemy.

I wondered what the difference was between Theophilos and these others. Were they more moral than he? Or would a more subdued personality type think a problem through and perhaps discover other avenues, where someone of Theophilos's strenuous temperament might see only one? I could only speculate on the answers at that point.

It was a fact of war that soldiers needed not only food, but women. In exchange for food, Theophilos provided the enemy with names of families whom he knew had young daughters. Because of their being shamed in this way in a society where virginity was prized, these young women were ruined for any kind of normal marriage and home life. Such a fate in a culture where strong family bonding was the key not only to happiness, but to survival, might well have been for some of them the kiss of death. Fathers and brothers did not forget, in all the intervening years, the person who was responsible for the shame of their daughters or sisters.

So in this community of strong male camaraderie – with the exception of Costas, an octopus fisherman, and a few foreigners who appreciated his intelligence and crusty wit – Theophilos was friendless.

*   *   *

It was July 1980, and the previous March, Theophilos had suffered a stroke that left him bedridden and paralyzed on his right side. I had been helping out by sitting with him three afternoons a week, so that his daughter, Sophia, could leave and take care of her farm chores. An hour or so after my arrival, after he wakened from his nap, he liked to have a glass of warm milk and bread. I went to the little kitchen located just off the bedroom.

A large refrigerator near the WC clicked on, and next to it the cement sink inlayed with mosaic chips caught a slow drip from the single iron faucet. On the adjacent wall stood an old wooden cabinet with white enamel counter and glass panes in the high cupboard doors. Inside, Theophilos kept a small supply of staples: bags of oregano and salt, a wine bottle half full of green olive oil, stoppered with a rolled up wad of waxed paper, and two bottles of Kambas *retzina*. In the freezer, stiff with frost, were five links of *lukániko* that, before his stroke, he liked to roast over the blue flame of the gas plate next to the sink. Below in the fridge, leftover macaroni sat congealed on a blue plate. I reached for the can of evaporated milk, its label graced with a picture of a Dutch woman nursing a baby.

Milk. When I went to Athens for art suppplies, I often had breakfast in a milk bar in Omonia Square. I especially favored the thick wedges of fresh yogurt, drizzled with honey, but the other customers – mostly men – drank hot milk served in thick glasses with a hard roll on the side. From early childhood Greeks have warm milk and bread every morning for breakfast. Over the years, each customer had adopted his own style: one broke bread into the hot milk, often tinted a pale brown with Turkish coffee, and spooned it into his mouth. Another buttered his bread, took a bite, then a sip from the glass, mixing the two before swallowing. Whatever their individual styles, they shared a similar relish in and concentration on the task at hand.

I remembered these men as I mixed the evaporated milk with water and heated it over the gas burner for Theophilos. After it warmed I poured the milk over bread broken up in the glass and tested a drop on my wrist. Back at his bedside, I fed him spoonful by spoonful. As his toothless gums worked at the soggy mass, his eyes took on that same concentration of the men in the milk bar.

What were they, what is he feeling? I tried to imagine what bits of childhood memories might be stirring in their unconscious minds that might cause such a darkening of eyes in so intense a concentration. The men in the milk bar were hungry for their breakfasts; and

Theophilos was hungry too. It could be as elementary as that. But I wondered if they were hungry as well for a little bit of softness, for a chance to take off that interminable mask of machismo, and to imagine themselves back in their mother's kitchens – or even at her breast, that brief, ecstatic comfort of infancy – that it might relieve them of the awesome responsibility of lives that held no guarantees of happiness and that, no matter how tough their bodies or how careful their choices, would end for each of them, without exception, in death.

*   *   *

He was afraid of the night. While the whole town snored in its collective dream, Theophilos lay on his sickbed, eyes open, eyes that refused to close until the first rays of morning began to filter through the shutters. He lay staring at his window, waiting for light. The naked bulb above him illuminated the room, but it did not erase shadows. Because of the shadows, he had to have someone there with him all through the night. Every night. It was his daughter, Sophia, usually, and on the other evenings a young tourist from California came in from her day at the beach to earn extra money.

Theophilos was afraid of the night. If someone was there, he could control his thoughts, could distract them from the subject that refused to give him rest. If someone was there, death could not come suddenly on velvet feet and snatch him away in the night.

*   *   *

They had been asking him for weeks, and he always had just the one answer: he closed his eyes, raised his eyebrows and chin – the emphatic and silent gesture, "No," definite and inviolable. Once when I had stopped at his shop to say hello, he told me that priests were *malákes* (a common insult, meaning "masturbators"). A procession from one of the churches had just passed in commemoration of a holiday, and Theophilos was telling me it was all foolishness, that everything connected with the church was for the weak and was to him nonsense.

So the answer was the same for all who asked – his daughter, his sister, Altheia, and finally his son, Alexandros. They asked him if he wanted to see a priest so he could make his confession and receive the sacrament, and they all got the same response: "No."

*   *   *

Five o'clock on an August afternoon: another day, just like the last one hundred fifty since his stroke, identical, predictable, inevitable, another dreary day grinding down into its final hours.

Alexandros arrived with Soula, the town clerk. It was Saturday, her day off, and she was in a print housedress, as if Alexandros had abducted her from the midst of her chores. A sense of urgency entered with the two; there was little time left, this business of the will had to be accomplished now, or it might never get done.

I was told I did not have to leave the house, so I sat in the kitchen. Alexandros's gruff voice carried easily from the next room, and he made no attempt to quiet it.

"We are here to write your will, Babá. Soula has come to copy down what you say. So. We will begin. The farm, start with the farm, Babá."

With the disposition of each piece of property, Theophilos's voice had become more and more tearful. I could only imagine how he must have felt as all that he had worked for his entire life – a shop here, a bit of land there, a house in the *hóra* – was turned over to his family. The stroke had made him bedridden, but had not diminished his spirit much. But now, it was as if one more part of his life had been skinned away, leaving only the tender dermis, raw and smarting. His world, he himself was drying up and shrinking as each bit was torn away. His world? These four bare walls. And " 'Ákros?" Reduced to this fragile form beneath a white sheet that all too soon would become his shroud.

Not only that, but Alexandros and his wife, his grandchildren and Sophia too, were burdened by him. He knew this well; he could see it in their faces, hear it in the way they spoke to him. Of his whole family, only his sister Altheia came daily and talked sweetly with him, tenderly stroking the numbed hand where it lay on his chest.

Alexandros instructed Soula to help his father make his mark on the paper. That accomplished, Theophilos sighed, "I am finished. Leave me alone."

After his son and the clerk left, he allowed the tears to fall. Where had it all gone? It was as if he had died without really leaving the world, but was instead forced to behold the poverty of his life at the time when all he had placed his trust in vanished before his eyes. In a puff of breath, his last breath, everything he'd identified himself with and sacrificed for would pass – had, in essence, already passed from him – and he, " 'Ákros," was no more, and would never again be repeated.

"I am a dying man." He sighed to me. "When I go, that will be it. Kaput."

It was lame bravado. A holdover from his younger days when he could look at the meaning of life and not be cowed by the nihilism he gave to it. But now the grief that lingered in back of his eyes spoke of longing, a yearning for comfort in this one final struggle.

"For the body, perhaps, that is true." I hesitated. "But some claim our souls continue."

Theophilos closed his sad eyes and didn't say a word.

*   *   *

From one side of the sleeping man's bed Sophia hissed fiercely to Alexandros that she'd had it up to here, that she needed help and she needed it now, that not one more day could she go on bearing the full burden of caring for their father, that Petros was complaining the farm was falling to ruin; that Alexandros had to contribute more time, make sacrifices too, that his father didn't die every day of the week, that she was going without rest every hour of the night and day, and in this heat; and look at her hair (she pulled a few wiry, whitened strands out from under the stiff nylon scarf) and the new lines, she was growing old before her time (she looked at me for corroboration, knowing we were the same age); that if she didn't spend more time at the farm Petros would seduce one of the tourists he took in his *caique* to the beaches, that Petros was a handsome man and besides, she had always suspected he was unfaithful to her, so she wouldn't be surprised; and that, Virgin Mary, if she didn't get some relief soon, she would collapse from exhaustion and her marriage would be destroyed; and that was the whole truth of it!

In a hoarse whisper from the opposite side of the bed, Alexandros asked Sophia just what she expected him to do; that here they were right in the middle of the tourist season, that his hotel was filled and booked through September; and not only that, but he must tend the shop as well; that he was there in the mornings to shave his father; that his aunt was always complaining too, accusing him of favoring his business over his own dying father; but what was he to do; the tourists come, the tourists go, they must sleep somewhere; was he supposed to turn them away; that did she realize how much money he would lose if he closed for just *one day;* that he had mouths to feed, was responsible to his family first of all, and his wife was too busy with the children and her own shop to help, so just what did Sophia expect him to do when he could do no more; that who knew how long their father would last, it could be months yet; that he could stand no more complaints, in fact, would tolerate no more complaints; that she was the daughter, that it was her duty to tend their sick father and that was his last word on the subject!

*   *   *

The next afternoon Theophilos and his friend, Costas, were talking quietly when Alexandros burst in and, without amenities, announced that he thouught the best thing was for his father to go into a hospital in Athens. Theophilos remained silent, looking down at his immobile hand as Alexandros recited the various advantages of his proposition – the better care, the skilled help available in case of emergency. His gruff voice showed no hint of warmth, only relief and urgency, as if he had just rounded a bend after a long and arduous trek and, spotting the smoke curling from the chimneys of his village, experienced the relief of homecoming at the same moment he quickened his pace and continued with renewed vigor. As the eldest son of the dying man, he had become the head of the family. As the head of the family, he expected his commandments to be met unquestioningly.

Sophia arrived from the farm, and Alexandros explained once again that he had arrived at a solution to all their problems, that their father should go to a hospital in Athens where he could get expert care (he looked at his father's quiet face), "And when you are well, you can come back home, Babá."

We all watched Theophilos. There was a long pause. "Whatever you want," he said with a bewildered look mixed with resignation.

When I think of Theophilos's face, I remember how much Alexandros resembled his father – thick, wavy hair, the strong jaw – and I realize that, like his father, Alexandros, too, was a man of few choices. Within this sense of limitation a person is, in a way, cornered. Escape depends upon an almost predatory view of others that sooner or later will claim its victim. And, if Theophilos's experience was any model to go by, the process ultimately involved the victimization of the predator as well.

But free will cannot function when there is perception of only one choice. I asked myself, was someone who was aware of only one choice, who, due to temperment, upbringing, environmental factors, tradition or whatever, was incapable of perceiving alternatives for any reason – was that person culpable for the evil he or she contributed to the world? Even abundant choice did not guarantee right choice. No. It was more an intuitive, as opposed to instinctual thing, an *intelligence of the heart* that seemed to be the key here, that made the choices we did make – responsible.

And even then, we often weren't sure.

Sophia had remained uncharacteristically silent, her face reflecting the conflict within, her eyes never leaving the face of her father during Alexandros's entire discourse. After a pause, she straightened her shoulders as if coming out of a dream and said quietly, "No. He will stay here."

*   *   *

Theophilos told me he wanted to see Tom, Andreaus and my friend from the States, who had been here a month and would be leaving the next day. So that night on our way to his goodbye dinner with friends, we stopped to visit Theophilos. Tom was an ordained minister, but spent most of his time as an administrator in a small liberal arts college. Far from the somber cleric, he was lighthearted and positive, comfortable to be around, a good guy, not like a *papás* at all, the Greeks said.

I left the two of them alone and sat in the courtyard outside. After five or ten minutes Tom came out looking perplexed. He was having trouble understanding Theophilos, who for months now could no longer wear his false teeth. Would I come in and help?

I had no luck either, and in frustration, Theophilos gave up and closed his eyes, raising his chin in that emphatic "No."

"Never mind, it doesn't matter," he added bluntly.

On the walk to the dinner it occured to us that Theophilos might have wanted to make the confession so long sought by his family. He must have asked to see Tom, not only as a friend, but also in his capacity as a *papás*. And now he refused to speak! Tom agreed that might be the reason Theophilos had been so abrupt with us when we had failed to understand him. We would stop by that evening after dinner, he said. And if Theophilos was awake, they would have their talk.

But he was asleep, Sophia said later when we passed by. She dared not waken him, as he got so little sleep, and she had so few respites from his demands. We didn't say why we had come.

I was awake until morning. A friend was going to die without having made his peace. He wouldn't see a Greek *papás*, and in a few hours Tom would board the early plane to Athens and New York. Theophilos's tormented soul weighed on my own deep into the night.

I knew what had to be done; but in that fearful, secret place that valued the opinions of others, I just didn't want to do it. Yet, in another part of me, perhaps a deeper, more ancient one, I felt compelled, as if someone were holding blinders to the sides of my head, obscuring the feared distractions, so that I would go, like a horse, forward toward some goal.

At the same time I knew I had a choice. Like the horse, I could dig in my heels and not move. Or I could simply ignore the impulse and go my own way. Or even go to the *papás* myself and tell him that Theophilos was ready, maybe not to see *him*, but at least he was ready to confess. And what if that backfired?

I didn't know anything about confession. And not being a Catholic, I was never terribly comfortable in confessing to wrongdoings, much less listening to a recital of someone else's.

But in all my objections, the only thing revealed was my fear. I was afraid – afraid I would fail, and that all this agonizing was just spiritual pride and self-deception of a misguided fool awash in piety. Afraid, yes, of looking foolish, that it would get around that Anna had tried to convert " 'Ákros," ha, ha, ha, ha.

But there was so little time, no time, actually, for the luxury of weighing the factors. So little time to even think of how to proceed. In a little over a week I too would be leaving the island.

I remembered a book sent to me a few years before. There was a prayer in it that might serve in this case. I found the book and the passage:

> Father, I come before thee with a humble heart, thy broken and grieving child. I have sinned against society and against you. Now, at the eleventh hour, I turn to you with pain and anguish in my heart, for I see that my entire life has been spent in defiance of you. Father, if thou art merciful as the Scriptures say, forgive me, for I have sinned mightily and am truly sorry.

Yes, it would do. I translated it into my rudimentary Greek and tried to memorize it so I wouldn't falter when it came time to lead Theophilos in the prayer.

By 12:45 the next afternoon, I felt confident enough to walk into town and down the narrow, winding streets to his house.

But Sophia's hurried instructions as to what Theophilos would be needing that afternoon were all it took to wipe my mind clean. All I had memorized just hours before vanished. I could hear only the voice of Sophia talking loudly to neighbors as she passed down the street and out of earshot around a corner. Then there was silence.

*   *   *

I sat on the cane-seated chair by the side of the bed. A soft, almost submarine light pierced the shutters of the sickroom from the whitewashed street, blazing in trembling midday heat. The room was cool and smelled faintly of the alcohol that Sophia had rubbed on his back to calm the chafed skin. Theophilos was sleeping, hands resting lightly on his chest. I was having trouble keeping my eyes open and finally yielded to the temptation to dare rest my head on the edge of his pillow. In a few seconds I, too, was asleep.

Moments later, we both wakened. We greeted each other, and Theophilos told me he had just enjoyed the sweetest of sleeps. I smiled at the gentle flirtation, and informed him that Tom left early that morning and had asked me to say goodbye. Then I moved right into it, afraid I would lose my nerve.

"Theophilae, last night, when Tom and I were here, had you wanted to make a confession?"

"Yes." He said with a nod.

So far, so good, I thought. At least we weren't mistaken about that. "Well," I fumbled for the words, "if you wanted to do it now, it would be all right. What I mean is that you . . . you don't need a *papás*. God is here; Cristos is here in this room. We can't see him, but he is here, listening, and he can be your priest, Theophilae. Do you believe that?"

"Yes," he said quietly, to my surprise.

"Well, then, can you talk to Cristos? Can . . . you tell him the bad things you have done?"

He turned his head away. "But, there is so much, so many bad things," he said, his eyes taking on that look of hopeless resignation I had witnessed so much lately. "I wouldn't know where to begin; it's too late."

"No, it's not too late, Theophilae. And if there is too much, there might be a remedy for that. Just think of the worst thing you have done, the one thing that has given you the most fear and guilt. Tell that one, Theophilae, and it will carry with it all the rest." This thought tumbled out into words effortlessly and with conviction – a small grace that left me surprised again, and grateful.

He started to speak, haltingly at first, and then the words gained momentum until, at last, it was all out, the great, horrendous deed that Theophilos had lived with nearly his entire adult life.

But I could only assume this was true, for it was the same for me as for Tom the previous evening: I hadn't understood a word of what he said.

"Do you understand?" he asked.

"Yes," I said simply, knowing at that moment that it wasn't important that I understood his words. Because, if he had directed those undecipherable words of his confession to me, what happened next was directed only to God: one tear spilled onto his left cheek, and another, as Theophilos slowly gave in to the outpouring of his remorse.

"Forgive me, I am sorry, forgive me, forgive me," he said again and again to God through his tears, as the innumerable sins of a lifetime were washed away.

My tears, too, welled up, as I felt with awe and humility the significance of what was taking place, as if nothing else mattered that summer, but this one, single moment. That even though Tom and I had failed the night before, whatever power it was that guarded souls had taken over, and had caused the little speeches, the "thee's" and "thou's," and the rote prayers to vanish. In their place had come simple words that had somehow opened the way for this man, so burdened with guilt and fear, to receive his peace.

It was almost as if we had been puppets, willing to have our strings pulled. No. Not puppets. More like the hand fulfilling the function that the brain imparts to it. I had been willing to be a hand of God. Simply willing. In his way, so had Theophilos. And in that willingness alone, the hands had suddenly discovered their relationship to the brain – and to each other.

"You are clean now, Theophilae," I told him when he was calm again. "You can sleep at night now without fear."

*　*　*

Two days later Sophia gushed to me how her father had slept both nights through, and how she, too, had gotten the first rest in his house since his stroke. I explained what had happened, that Theophilos had made his confession, and how I thought he had experienced forgiveness. I was not sure she understood my battered Greek enough to fully grasp the import of what had happened.

But a few days later, close to the time I would be leaving them to devote all my time to packing and mailing for departure, Sophia had a dream.

The dream took place in the enclosure where *panagíris* were held – a long, low building, whitewashed outside and in, with a white cement table and white benches down its entire length. A completely white room. On the eve of a particular saint's nameday, liturgies were held in all the churches named after that saint. Later, the *panagíri* feast was held in the whitewashed enclosure nearby, with abundant food, wine, and music. In her dream, Sophia had entered one of these enclosures to find her father seated alone at the end of a table that was covered with plates of food of all description – a banquet spread before him over the entire table. Theophilos, sitting tall and calm in his place of honor, looked at his daughter and said to her:

"You, too, Sophia, can take part in the feast."

A week later, late in the afternoon on a hot, unseasonably still afternoon in August, Theophilos died. I stopped by later that evening to attend the wake.

His flower-covered body lay in a blue casket in the parlor of the three-room house. In his long, beautiful hands rested a small icon of Christ.

I sat next to his nephew. But there was little to say, only thoughts of the previous weeks, a sense of peace, joy for Theophilos.

The next morning I caught the 7:30 plane to Athens for my connecting flight to the U.S. At 5:30 Greek time, I saw the toy towers of the New York World Trade Center rising up out of the immense, blue Atlantic. Back on the island, twenty-four hours after his death, I knew Theophilos's body was being lowered into the ground, and the first clods of the soil from which his physical body had once emerged were being thrown over him, one by one, by his family.

Chapter Nine
White

"You would know our Lord's meaning in this thing?
Know it well. Love was his meaning. Who showed it you?
Love. What did he show you? Love.
Why did he show it? For love."
                                              – Julian of Norwich

1. Tourist

THE SIXTH DAY BACK IN GREECE, AND ALL OF THEM cleaning and airing the house. I had spent the winter in the States, where, after an absence of ten years, I'd "tested the waters" of employment and housing. Now it was June, and I had returned to the island to pack up the last of my belongings. I had to make my departure in shifts, it seemed, the slow tearing away of the butterfly's wings.

The house had been soaked through completely by a particularly rainy winter. The smell of mildew oozed from the pores of white walls, gone gray from dampness. Last year's sandals left in the cupboard were fleshed out in a fur of green mold. The same with some of the paintings and books in the studio. I washed everything off with vinegar water and rubbed the paintings with stale bread. But the books especially were too far gone to save. I was sad to lose them, knowing I would probably never buy replacements. These books had been nice to have, to drop in and visit with occasionally, like old friends, familiar and reassuring, as much as a memoir about this time is familiar and reassuring – an old friend, and equally hard to say goodbye to.

Everyone told me what an awful winter it had been. Incessant rains and nor'easters grounded planes and delayed boats from the mainland. Many old people had died, and winters never were very kind to cats on the island. I had a hunch that Kalliope hadn't survived this one; she still hadn't shown up as she usually did, slinking over the wall opposite the house, scolding at the half stranger who smelled of the city and who had a city-wound spring coiled in the pit of her stomach. I would miss Kalliope, my little companion.

The odor of mildew and mothballs pervaded every room, and a film of dust gritted all the surfaces – even, I noticed to my surprise, the vertical ones, which had been clean and dry when I left six months before. The cabinet where I kept clothes, a large chest full of blankets and pillows, the kitchen stove, curtains enclosing a makeshift closet, bookshelves, the very walls themselves were covered in it: the normal dust of a winter's closing, turned to mud by the excessive humidity.

I scrubbed the surfaces, and re-scrubbed until I discovered that what looked clean while wet, carried all manner of imaginative dirty streaks when dry. So again, a third time, I wiped with fresh water and clean sponge, the task seemingly endless – dreary, dull work that necessitated repeated trips to the well for buckets of fresh water. I worked slowly, retreating during the hottest part of the day to my bed to read and nap. The bed – an island of order in the midst of a chaotic sea of gritty furniture and swept-up rubble. And everywhere, and for weeks, the taint of mildew would linger until the first blast of July's windy heat carried it all off to Africa.

Aside from the familiar drudgery of spring cleaning, I had to admit that it felt strange being back. This strangeness was partly a feature of jet-age travel – a lethargy still clothed in the noisy traffic of St. Paul, last minute preparations and warm, clucking farewells of friends, and all wrapped in the assurance that I would be returning in just two and a half months. It seemed my mind hadn't caught up with my body, and though I was not yet totally here in mind and spirit, I could still say that I had seldom been more present.

It was as if my decision to begin a new life in the States had stripped away finally the last remnants of illusion about the life here, as if I had already said my goodbyes, the really heartfelt ones, the previous summer. And so I thought I had. Returning to tie up the final strings was like being a tourist again, but a rather world-weary one who had seen it all before and was no longer enchanted by delightful villages and who longed to become rooted somewhere, settled down into the mundane, which, paradoxically, had suddenly become exciting, untested and pregnant with new possibilities.

It was true. I had become bored here. Bored with the life cycle of tourism that had taken over the more natural rhythms of my earlier years on the island. Bored with the town whose culture had been increasingly compromised by the demands of visitors, blaring through its nights the monotonous cadence of the disco beat coming from a growing number of bars and nightclubs. Bored certainly with the proliferation of cars and the speedy life they brought with them. Rushing seemed more appropriate to the place I had just come from than to Mykonos, where the *modis operandi* had never been speed, but patience and a measured, relaxed encounter with the task at hand.

There was also some disillusionment with what at first appeared to be a new shallowness in my relationships with other foreigners who lived here – a condition that revealed itself subtly, yet, it seemed, concurrently with the announcement of my plans to move back to the States. The old intimacy of winters shared gave way to a reserve that was unsettling and left me longing for family – they, at least so far, remained the same, were always there, back there.

But it was not unusual, this reserve, I think. With so many people coming and going, I might have become just another tourist, not only to myself, but maybe to my friends as well. I knew the feeling well enough to empathize. I, too, had tired of the unending leavetakings of visitors during the summer. People from New York or St. Paul or California came through; we would have dinner, a day at the beach, and then they would be off to their next destination. Little time to sustain deep relationships under such conditions when the other party was always leaving.

And so it might have been with my own impending departure; foreign friends living permanently on the island seemed to withdraw a little, perhaps seeing me as part of the other culture again, while they were staying where they were, just as I had experienced it in waving off my visitors. That thin, almost invisible wall between people who were once close . . . and the feeling of desertion, perhaps on both sides.

I had many departure-type things to do – boxes of books to pack, as well as the ordeal of parceling up paintings and art supplies for shipment. Decisions had to be made on what to take and what to leave of the many mementos accumulated in ten years – mementos from friends who had left before me, or from the string bag I took on walks, filled with objects left anonymously by wind and sea or passing being, captured in the bag and placed on a shelf or in a corner of a room, imbued with meaning by me, for me.

There was the stone collection – remnants from beaches all over Greece. And hand-braided rugs from Audrey, an American friend who had left three years before. The *caíque* model made by the town blacksmith after he retired. And so much more. What to take and what to leave? The decisions were too hard, cut too close to the bone of the ending of all this.

But there was plenty of time. I could avoid the pain and drudgery of packing for a while. I would become a tourist again, escape to the beaches and spend a lazy month working not on painting or packing, but on my tan and enjoying the lingering lunches with friends in the shade of open-air restaurants by the sea. If I felt like a tourist, I might as well enjoy the island like one.

While my non-Greek friends seemed to withdraw into their own lives, the Greeks were different. Perhaps it was *filótimo*, that curious selflessness upon which their strong and complex sense of self worth depended. The Greeks gave – without effort it sometimes seemed – of their bounty, their homes, their lives, their affection.

There was Dimitri, who had helped with the *hierosphýia* at my friend Andreaus' farm the previous year. Once, about five years into my stay, I went to buy groceries at his son's store. Dimitri stood outside by the vegetable stand, figuring the totals on a calculator sitting before him. His Athenian customer nodded toward me and asked who the foreigner was (my greeting to him in Greek had caught her attention). Dimitri answered in the colloquial:

"*Dikyiá más, 'éine.*" Our own. An idiom that evoked feelings of warmth and familiarity – a step beyond saying merely "*Ménei 'edó.*" She lives here.

The day before I left the island for good, I went to say goodbye. Dimitri gave me a big bear hug and wished me a safe trip, and that good health be granted to all of us until I could return for a visit.

And there were Andonis and Irini, my neighbors across the road. I sometimes bought cheese and eggs from them, and often they gave me additional vegetables from their garden, an extra cheese or an egg or two.

Still tall and powerful at seventy-six, Andonis's most prominent sign of age was the loss of nearly every tooth in his mouth.

"Ah, Anna," he said one morning when he had stopped by to pass a little time, which he did at least once a week. "What will we do without you? It won't be the same having a stranger in this house."

I said I would miss him too, that he had been a good friend. I promised to come back and see him and Irini one day. What lay unspoken between us, beyond the sincerity of our intentions, was the reality that we both knew to be true: that after I left, we would probably never lay eyes on each other again. But the words of regret had been said and heartfelt claims of affection exchanged, and these were important gestures and would warm me in the years ahead, whatever those years would bring.

And their humor. To be inspired to laugh at oneself was a true gift. As our conversation shifted to the trip itself, Andonis sat forward.

"How long does the plane take to *Néo Yórki*?" He asked.

"About nine hours. I leave August third at noon."

"And what time will you arrive?"

"About five in the afternoon." I knew what was coming. Though uneducated, Andonis was intelligent. I knew that his intrinsic common sense had gotten tripped up by the paradox emerging in our conversation.

"If you leave at noon and get in at five in the afternoon, how can it take nine hours?" he asked, shrugging his broad shoulders and leaning forward on his cane, waiting for my answer.

"Because in different parts of the world it is different times of the day – the sun's position changes," I said, and held my closed fist up to the sun. "See how the sun hits my hand on one side only, and it's day, while the other side is in shadow, and it's night. Now when my airplane flies west . . . "

On I went, warming to my subject from his attention, which appeared to be rapt. Suddenly he interrupted me in mid-sentence.

"Anna, those teeth, are they yours?"

It had been the Greeks whom I had come to get to know on that first short trip back in 1967 when I had stayed ten days before moving on to Kazantzakis's birthplace on the island of Crete. And it would be the Greeks again whose earthy wisdom and matter-of-fact honesty (which sometimes felt as harsh as the stony landscape that spawned them) had opened me and re-formed me in the ten years I had been their guest. And it would be the Greeks whose generosity and affection had healed me, and who would provide me with the most heartfelt and poignant farewell.

✳   ✳   ✳

And finally the task of cleaning my house for this last part of my sojourn was done. My kitchen was clean and the walls, freshly whitewashed, glowed in warm lamplight as I cooked a simple meal of zucchini, onions, tomatoes and eggs. I took the plate of food out to the terrace and ate slowly, sipping *retzina*, holding the moment of pleasure a long time. The eggs and vegetables satisfied completely, and I sat listening to the evening sounds, the few frogs left down the road in the shrinking pond, the cows' murmur, sounds of their heavy shuffle in the dust floating across fields, a child's laugh – all these sounds – and I, silent, sitting here wrapped up in that breathless rose light that deepened and deepened until it finally enfolded us all in the indigo blanket of a warm June night.

I had forgotten about that light. I had forgotten the numberless evenings I'd sat on the same terrace, alone or with friends, watching it change, wrapped in that expanse of rose gold light. That night, with the heavy labor of cleaning over at last, I could feel something inside begin to loosen, that chronic knot I never knew I had until I came to Greece, and it disappeared. This night on the terrace I could feel it loosen, thread by thread, so that it seemed as if I had just swollen up by taking in some of what was around me, and what was around me had taken in some of me – a kind of psychic orgasm, where there was no separation, no barrier between figure and ground. As if the universe had been trying to tell me something: that in reality there were no barriers, no barriers at all and most of all no barriers to light, no more to learn about, but light. The entire sojourn had been given me to learn about *Light*. It only remained for all the other distractions to be stripped away gradually, like the muddy streaks of winter grime scrubbed layer after layer from my furniture.

What was this light, this peculiar vast openness that etched all things in its clear beam? At its most intense, it repelled life and sent it scurrying for shelter. It was light that could blind me if I looked at it directly. And it could kill if I became dazzled by it and, in confusion, walked off a cliff. But there were times, at its beginning and at its end – when its illumination was at its weakest by ordinary standards – that it held its most secret power and the most nourishment for me – and for others beholding it.

2. Delos

It was August, a few years before this radiant evening on the terrace; the *hóra* and all the island beaches were reeling under the demands of the high tourist season. Brenda, an American friend, and I decided to escape for a couple days and spend the night of the full moon on neighboring Delos. We barely had time for a quick breakfast on the harbor before taking off with a small number of groggy tourists who had signed on for the morning tour of that island. As our *caïque* cast off, the sea was already beginning to churn with the awakening of the day's *Meltemi*. Farther out in the open sea, we pitched and rolled in swells that broke under the gunwales in a green, hissing froth. I noticed that a few of the passengers had suddenly become subdued. As their faces took on a sickly pale hue, one by one they lurched to the railing. Brenda seemed immune to queasiness, but all I had to do was look at one of these people and the power of suggestion succeeded where the rising and falling horizon beyond the stern had so far failed. I took my turn at the rail with the rest, ending in a series of racking, dry heaves that left me weak and exhausted.

But arrival in the quieter waters of the protected harbor of Delos always revived me on these trips, and by the time I actually set foot on land, I had recovered. We had arrived at last at the sacred island of light.

The recorded history of Delos goes back as far as the tenth century B.C. Well known in ancient times as the site of the Delia Festival, it happened to be the bark from Delos rounding Cape Sounian that signaled Socrates' taking of the hemlock. The tiny island was also a great commercial port, situated in the center of trade routes between the eastern and western worlds. Since the time of the two purges, both for religious and political reasons in the fifth and second centuries B.C., no one had been able to claim citizenship, and in modern times, no one but the ruin guards and their families had been allowed to live here.

On our way to book a room, Brenda and I walked through the square where once thousands of slaves had been traded in a day. Then, passing through the orderly ruins of the sacred temple of Apollo and past the elevated phalluses of the Cult of Dionysius (favorite leaning posts for tourist snapshots), we arrived at last at the small adobe-colored hotel. Litza, the proprietor, welcomed us and gave us a room. We left our bags and soon joined the rest of the tourists spreading out into the ruins like ants scurrying among grains of sand.

There was little left of the structures of ancient Delos. Centuries of neglect and sacking by invading armies had relieved the island of most of its once renowned splendor. What was left that could be moved was picked through by the early settlers of Mykonos; today, anyone walking the streets of the *hóra* could admire the elaborately carved lintels and the time-smoothed marble staircases of its oldest houses. What remained on *Delos* that hadn't been stolen, put in museums, or incorporated into the architecture of Mykonos, were mere remnants – scrolled cornices and pediments mismatched to prone, wind-softened columns. A few wealthy merchants' houses, their ancient mosaic floors protected by twentieth-century roofs, stood on the outskirts of the town; six of the lions, whose Naxian marble details were smoothed to a pitted patina by the elements, still guarded the Sacred Way leading to the Temple of Apollo.

Delos was the legendary birthplace of the god, Apollo. The myth tells of his immortal and philandering father, Zeus, who one day impregnated the mortal, Leto. She was then banished by Zeus's angry wife, Hera, to wander aimlessly without a home forever. In her wanderings she came upon a barren rock of an island that floated, as she did in her exile, without anchor on the surface of the sea. Zeus promised to allow his new child to become the island's protector if Leto could give birth there when her time came. He named the island Delos and then caused four columns to rise from the bottom of the sea, stabilizing the island upon them in the spot where it is today, near the center of the Cycladic archipelago. Attended in her labor by the Nine Muses of the arts, Leto gave birth to twins: Artemis, Goddess of the Hunt and Apollo, most beloved of all the pantheon, God of the Sun.

Apollo: both human and divine, whose light, the sun, illuminated the entire world and gave it life, whose vision dispelled darkness, who brought healing and restoration and enlightenment. Apollo, the Classical Age's precursor to Christ, also human and divine and of humble birth who, centuries later, would promise similar healing in a vastly different world.

On Apollo's island, it was hard not to feel the cumulative effects of century after century of veneration. It seemed as if there were a presence in the very stones of the walkway and in the ruins of houses that lined the narrow, winding streets. The presence was evident, too, in the wildflowers of Delos, bright with scarlet poppies high as a person's thighs, violet-colored thistles big as coffee cups and purple statice as tall and thickly sown as the meadow grass in which it grew. Over and above them all, the stately Queen Anne's Lace bowed regally in the wind, large as dinner plates, each tiny blossom that composed it an image of the whole flower. It was as if the sunlight in this place had a magic growth elixir that was lacking in the atmosphere of Mykonos, say, or Tinos, or Paros or Naxos.

At twelve-thirty the tourists left for Mykonos. Brenda and I collected our lunch and hiked through the ruins to Fourni, a small beach on the southwest corner of the island. With not a soul in sight, we stripped to our skins and with snorkel and masks plunged into the sea. For a half hour, we floated and bobbed like porpoises in the salty water, diving under to catch a look at the undersea flora and fauna. Around us the Aegean shimmered in the midday sun's rays that were bent and detonated into flickering colors by the watery prism. We lunched on canned mackerel and crackers, hard boiled eggs, peaches and water. Then, oiled up, we browned like roasts in the cove we had found sheltered from the wind. As the sun lowered to the west and it got cooler, we napped. Then another swim and the long hike back over stubbly fields and crumbling dry-stone walls, all the time keeping a wary eye open for the skittish vipers who came out to hunt at that time of day. After a welcome shower at the hotel and a change of clothes, we hiked up Cynthus, the small mountain, to watch the sun go down.

Mount Cynthus, only about four hundred feet in elevation, nevertheless was the highest point on the island. At its summit was the site of the ancient temple of Zeus, Apollo's father and head of the pantheon. All that was left to mark it were remnants of a mosaic plaque. To the east, a full moon rose huge and silent over Mykonos. To the west, sinking with a steady majesty, Apollo, red as his island's poppies, sizzled into the now still sea.

The wind had died, as it often did in the evenings during the *Meltemi* season. Relieved of its incessant howl, the landscape and all who dwelt in it relaxed, no longer needing to fight it, no resistance, only just the letting go. And with the letting go, the new sensitivity to sound: to the now audible din of insects, the cackle of goats, the tremolo of sheeps' bells on the far hillside. To the hum of the heavens where stars were just emerging that would no longer be obliterated by the dust whipped up by the wind and that hung like baubles, large, close, reachable perhaps. I knew, as we turned to leave that place, that I wanted to sleep there, alone on the mountain, under those stars.

Back on the hotel terrace, we had an *ouzo* and talked with Yiorgos and Nikos, two of the guards living on the island. Soon Litza was there with plates of stewed wild rabbit, swimming in a savory gravy with onions, crisp fried potatoes and a bottle of *retzina* to wash it all down.

It was on our after-dinner walk through the ruins that I heard the children's laughter. Above us the full moon played its ghostly pale light along the winding streets and partially restored houses of ancient Delos. We walked slowly; there was no hurry. The theater had been there thousands of years; it would not collapse before we got there.

We walked in that companionable intimacy of silence that is the hallmark of old friendships – not old in terms of time, necessarily, for I had known Brenda only four years. It was more an oldness of understanding, a feeling of comfort in the ranging of our own thoughts, without the nagging need to converse.

And then I heard it, trilling like a harp in high register. The laughter was there for a second and then gone. As if small urchins, living like paupers in the ruined houses, had seen the two of us coming and hidden themselves, tumbled over themselves, giggling in confusion. As if the ghosts of children remained in those old streets, spying on generations of visitors, ducking behind walls, peeking around corners, children caught in a time warp of eternal play. And Brenda had heard it once too, she told me later, on another moonlit night while walking alone among the ruins.

The theater rose out of the hillside from which it was carved. Tier upon tier, rising up and fanning out fifty to seventy-five feet from the circular stage at its base. To test the acoustics, Brenda dropped a safety pin on the stage, while I sat in the topmost tier, barely straining at all to hear the delicate ping of its impact reverberate upward.

We walked back to the hotel, where I collected my sleeping bag and flashlight. Brenda feared the mosquitoes would be bad outside and decided to sleep in our room. I set off alone on the approach to the steps leading up to the summit of Cynthos.

I had no idea where I would sleep. I knew that I didn't want to be near Zeus's temple site. It seemed too public there – used in a way. I needed something more remote, my own private place. I followed a path leading south on the summit. As I came out around a boulder and up onto a large granite hump, I found the perfect spot. Carved into the granite by the wind and rain were two hollowed out indentations. One of them was just large enough to stretch out in.

I was glad to have arrived at this place that seemed so peculiarly mine. I had no fear, either of being alone, or of the vipers that would be out roaming the heights in search of mice and lizards. In fact, I felt protected, as if the presence Brenda and I had always sensed on this island was on watch for the night. I squirmed into the sleeping bag and sat, arms around knees, looking out at the scene before me.

On three sides the slope dropped down to fields and ruins 350 feet below. To the east, across the still water, illuminated Mykonos winked like a silent carnival. Directly south, a rocky, crescent-shaped islet was decked with a light to warn off passing boats. Its beacon, brightly reflected in the still, black sea, seemed second in intensity only to the moon. Below the moon the nearby island of Rhenia brooded across from Delos harbor like some dark sea monster heaved up out of the deep.

I yawned, suddenly overcome with fatigue after all the fresh air, sun and good food. I slipped further down into the bag and soon slept.

There are two breezes that seem to herald the coming of the sun at dawn. The initial breeze occurs at the first blush of light in the eastern sky. At the moment of this subtle emergence of light, when all else is still in darkness, the first cock crows. An unsettling time, this transition between the darkness and light, when all is still obscured, except for that faintest of rose light touching the horizon. Unsettling, as all transition times are unsettling, a time of subtle tension and upheaval embodied in the breeze and announced by the cock's call.

Needless to say, it is the earth's motion that reveals the sun, as much as it can be said that the sun's arrival reveals the earth. As to which comes first, though, the breeze, the blush of pink or the cock's crow, I have never known. But of the three, it is the breeze and the light that interest me, their congruence, the seeming dependence of the sun's arrival on a terrestrial disturbance of the atmosphere. Or was the breeze dependent upon the arrival of the celestial body? The breath of the spirit bringing forth the light; or the light bringing forth the spirit?

Whatever the answer is, if there is, indeed, an answer to such musings, it was this ruffle of the first breeze that wakened me on the mountain around four-thirty the following morning. It curled around my ears and neck and made me shiver and pull the bag up closer around my head. Just as I was about to drop off to sleep again, I remembered I had wanted to wake up early to watch the sunrise.

To the west the full moon, huge and red as blood, was sinking toward the heights of Rhenia. When the moon was within seconds of breaking onto the horizon, the second breeze came up, a strong zephyr, bending the weeds beside me and tousling my hair. As the moon disappeared in a fading speck behind Rhenia, to the east over Mykonos the sun broke, its rays piercing over the headland and splashing radiance over the eastern slope of Cynthus.

Below, the light on the crescent-shaped islet had faded, no match for the intensity of the sun. Like humankind, this human-made object appeared puny and powerless in the light of Apollo's brilliance. Yet the moon, feminine and luminous, had ruled the heavens only a few hours before, had stood in all her majesty and power, Queen of the Night. But the moon could not light herself, and in the approaching light of the sun, she had faded rapidly before disappearing below the horizon. Then it was Apollo's moment, his light taking over with authority, enveloping, absorbing in its brilliance the blinking beacon below that vanished with the moon and, for the next several hours, would be seen no more.

*   *   *

3. Sacrament

In a sojourn that had once seemed used up of meaning, the sun itself appeared to hold the final surprise and continued to feed my mysterious longings. I had lived for ten years in a land strange to me. My path had crossed those of others belonging to that land, and I had been changed by the relationships we shared.

As I sat in the darkness of that first evening home in my clean house, I thought of the small shuttle plane that would take off in nine weeks and carry me from the baking tarmac of the island airport, above the surrounding hills to circle around and set its course for Athens. In my mind's eye I could see below me what I had seen many times before: the blazing white *hóra*, like a crocheted shawl the island women made, draped on the hills surrounding the turquoise circle of the small harbor. There would be people on the streets and inside buildings, many of them tourists, since it would be August. Iraklis, back for a visit, might be sitting in one of the cafes, or Andreaus, already hard at work framing up walls of the newest hotel. His mother, Eleni, would be dropping off homespun wool for Frascoula to knit into sweaters. In the walls of my vacant house, the ants would be storing up bits of grain for the winter. And in the stony ground, the remains of Yiorgos, Barba Manolis, Theophilos and eight kittens would be passively going about their task of becoming the generations of plant and animal life to follow.

But as the plane's altitude and distance increased, these little dots of life would disappear, become part of the houses, houses whose own individuality was vanishing into one solid, white shape against the ochre hillside.

It was as if our individual lives were enfolded – as the people were enfolded within the individual houses, and the houses into one main mass of white — as if every living thing were enfolded into some mysterious unity, just as we know the hues, red, orange, yellow, green, blue and violet are contained invisibly in the color white. As if the entire universe were contained invisibly in light.

And life, passing through that brief readjustment we call death, changed from a multiple to a singular substance, like the multiplicity of color traced back through a prism to its original state of pure light. The entire visible and invisible universe was composed of multiple expressions of some radiant and unfathomable unity.

And because of the nature of multiplicity, there was *relationship* between the individual parts. The nature of being "individual" was to relate — we could not do otherwise — with other humans, with plants, animals, with stones, the rain; to relate, as well, with what was unseen and unseeable, what seemed dead, what appeared evil. And, yes, with the sunlight. The sun: symbol of that mysterious unity from which everything evolved, with which it still seemed connected and to which it would ultimately return.

The nature of being alive was to relate, and our task was to celebrate that relatedness. To celebrate *and love* the process, because it was through this relating that *we were changed*: in celebrating and loving the process, we could only end up celebrating and loving that to which we related.

Birth and death were the transubstantiation. Life, and its myriad relationships, the sacrament.

*   *   *

Several weeks later, a few days before my departure from Greece, I returned with friends from a picnic on a secluded beach. We chugged along in a rented *caïque*, heading west, directly into the glare of the lowering sun. It sparkled on the surface of the sea like drops of water flung onto a hot, dry frying pan. At the base of steep cliffs jutting from the shoreline, a heat mist rose and continued along the horizon, even where there was no land in sight, blurring the line of demarcation between sky and sea.

We began to sing.

Nancy Raeburn grew up in Mahtomedi, Minnesota, a small community on the eastern shore of White Bear Lake just north of the Twin Cities. After returning from Greece, where she lived and painted for ten years, she received her Bachelor of Arts degree in English at Macalester College in 1984, that same year winning the Wendy Parrish Poetry Prize and Academy of American Poets College Prize. Her poetry has appeared in *The Beloit Poetry Journal* and *Studio One*. In 1991 excerpts from her book *Mykonos: A Memoir* were included in the anthology, *The House on Via Gombito: Writing by North American Women Abroad*, published by New Rivers Press.

Raeburn says of her writing: "I sought to express my Greek experience in new ways from the painting I had been doing those past ten years, and, since I had long kept a journal, writing seemed the most natural direction to go. A change of palette; a translation of color, form and texture into words. In the process, I discovered that the palettes were the same; only the substance differed, and that the elements of painting composition – balance, harmony, tension, repetition of patterns – apply to writing as well. Though there is generous room for overlap, writing seems to satisfy my hibernating, inward looking self, while painting appeals more to the extroverted side of my nature. I hope I never have to choose between them."